AFFIRM YOUR SELF

Day By Day

by

Suzanne E. Harrill, M.Ed., L.P.C.

AFFIRM YOUR
SELF
Day By Day

Copyright 1991 by Suzanne E. Harrill

Request for such permission should be addressed to:

Innerworks Publishing
2284 W. Holcombe, Suite 204
Houston, TX 77030

Cover Design by Diane Wilkinson at DiaGrammatics (713/666-0429)
ISBN: 0-9625996-1-1

A Letter

Dear Suzanne:
As I read these passages all those persons in me became conscious. The mother, the father, and the inner-child in me came to surface. We came together as we had never been before. We were a family unit within me and we read and shared as a union of souls.

My usual means of assimilating information was no longer sufficient. I felt compelled to absorb more than I was capable of internalizing. Answers to questions seemed to bounce off the page at me. I became controlled by an impulse that hungered for more and more information. My inner-self persuaded me to read on and on, and over and over again until the words and I became intimately connected.

You have honored me by sharing so much of yourself with me. I want to thank you for the experience. I have learned so much from you. Your insights into the human consciousness are far beyond printed words on a page. You are truly the essence of humanity. I am more for having read this.   *Sylvia*

Foreword

"Everyday is a new beginning." We smile at such a cliche not realizing the profound significance of the pure truth it contains, for through the darkness of night the old passes away and the light of dawn signifies a new day and a new life—if we capitalize on the opportunity.

An ancient teaching says that the beginning thought upon awakening sets the tone for the rest of the day. Considering this I was reminded of once watching and listening to a quartet preparing to sing. The leader hummed a note, a tone, and the others caught it and enthusiastically plunged into song on the same key, at the right pitch. They took advantage of a new beginning and issued forth a chorus of success—because they were in tune with the universal principle of harmony.

That's what this book is all about—getting a jump-start with the proper tone and pitch and continuing in the right rhythm throughout the day. Ralph Waldo Emerson wrote, "We are what we think about all day long...the good mind is known by the choice of what is positive, of what is advancing. We must embrace the affirmative." What do most of us think about all day long? Usually what we do not want rather than what we do, and the primary reason for this is a sense of unworthiness. We have forgotten who we are—the highest of creation and the completeness of the universe—heirs to all that which is good, true and beautiful. But with forgetting also comes remembering—a change of mind— and we have the power to choose that which is positive, of what is advancing. Day by day we can etch deeply in consciousness the truth of our being and transform our self-image and self-esteem, becoming new creatures on the side of life where wonders never cease.

The word "consciousness" is an enigma to many people, yet it is nothing more than the awareness, understanding and knowledge of our identity. And as this self-image expands to encompass our Spiritual Self, the attributes of that Self begin to be reflected in the phenomenal world and miracles become the order of the day. Just ask Suzanne Harrill. Suzanne is one of those practical Professional Counselors who blends intellectual expertise and spiritual understanding with the meaningful personal experiences of life. The result, or end-product, is a model for consciousness expansion—to help us realize our power through a deeper awareness, understanding and knowledge of who and what we truly are.

In *AFFIRM YOUR SELF Day by Day*, she takes us on a full year's course of New Beginnings—with delightful seed thoughts to plant in the garden of mind to change the way we think, to change our beliefs, thus changing our lives. Assume the role of the gardener and follow Suzanne's recommended sowing sequence. Let your mind be cultivated daily and water the seeds with fertile expectations, making sure that the weeds of trouble and discontent are continually uprooted. Do your part with dedication and enthusiasm, and a rich and bountiful harvest will be yours.

John Randolph Price
Author of *SUPER BEINGS* and
THE PLANETARY COMMISSION
Co-founder of The Quartus Foundation

Dedication

This book is dedicated to my Self and all people who have forgotten the importance of loving themselves. I dedicate this book with love to the potential in all humanity.

Suzanne Harrill

Acknowledgements

Creating this book was a group experience. I am grateful to my friends who helped and supported me. B. J. Callihan and Diane Langley spent hours typing and editing the manuscript. I also thank Carol Estes, Sylvia Salinas, and Jo Strauss for their help. Thank you to Beverly Threadgill for typesetting and page design. Thanks, too, to Diane Wilkinson for her beautiful cover design.

My very special thanks to Diane Langley, whose love and support enabled me to write this book. Without her labor of love, I could not have created such a finished piece of work.

Exceptions to the Copyright agreement:

Anyone who shares information in this book for teaching purposes or for personal growth has my permission to copy small portions of this book.

Please give credit to the author and give freely to others the Harrill Self-Esteem Indicator and the Twelve Steps of Building Self-Esteem.

Other Self-Esteem Products
by Suzanne E. Harrill

YOU COULD FEEL GOOD: A Self-Esteem Guide: Growing & Changing into your True Self. A self-help book which served as the source of many of the ideas used in this book *AFFIRM YOUR SELF DAY BY DAY.*

YOU COULD FEEL GOOD STUDY GUIDE. Eight lessons for group participation.

SELF-ESTEEM CARDS for Adults. Sixty card set including a wooden acorn to symbolize that each one of us is in the process of growing into our Full-Potential Self. There are pink affirmation cards, green suggestion cards, yellow definition cards and blue stumbling block cards.

CHILDREN'S SELF-ESTEEM CARDS. Forty cards with graphics plus star eraser which says "I Am a Star." Reverse side of cards provides information to parents and teachers on how to discuss concepts presented on the front of each card.

YOU COULD FEEL GOOD: BUILDING SOUND SELF-ESTEEM. A taped, live three-hour workshop on the topic of building self-esteem. Three cassette album.

AFFIRM YOUR SELF. Cassette tape of the Adult Self-Esteem Cards read aloud. Side two is a meditation.

BUILDING SELF-ESTEEM. Cassette tape of a one-hour lecture on Suzanne's approach to healing self-esteem.

Your bookstore can order these self-esteem products from New Leaf Distributing Company or you can write:

Innerworks Publishing
2284 W. Holcombe, #204
Houston, TX 77030
(713) 661-8284.

Introduction

This is a daily guide to help you learn to love and accept yourself. It will help you learn new patterns of thinking and feeling. When you learn to mature your fear thoughts and beliefs into love thoughts and beliefs, you experience a shift in how you feel. Wherever you are on your journey of self-discovery, use this daily guide to help you build a loving relationship with your Self.

Some of you are planting new seed thoughts that will take time to root and grow. Others may be further along and may use this guide as a reminder to stay on track. The concepts presented in this book build upon each other. If you begin using this book on any day of the year other than January 1, it may be necessary to backtrack a few days or a month to help the passage make sense.

A theme in this book is building self-esteem which is how you feel about yourself. Sound self-esteem is a place of feeling comfortable being who you are, your true Spiritual Self. When you allow your Spiritual Self to love you without conditions, you feel worthy, full of love, and able to pass it on to others.

You may want to take the Harrill Self-Esteem Indicator on the next page before you begin this book and then repeat the Indicator periodically to gauge your progress.

Many people have learned to open spiritually through the Twelve Step Programs. I have rewritten the Twelve Steps of Alcoholics Anonymous in holistic, present tense for those who would benefit from this approach for building self-esteem and loving yourself. It follows the Harrill Self-Esteem Indicator.

I would also like to encourage you to expand the love in your life to others by placing the name of a loved one, a friend, or a special person on the page corresponding to the day of their birth. You will then be able to include them in your focus for that day. The love in which

you are living and growing will then
radiate to all those within your world.

*Namasté,

Suzanne

*I honor the place in you of light, and
love, and truth, and beauty. When you
are in that place in you and I am in that
place in me, there is only one of us.

The Harrill Self-Esteem Indicator

This is a tool you may use to become more aware of and to evaluate your degree of self-esteem. It is not a test with right or wrong answers. Remember! You can feel better about yourself.

Answer the questions reflecting how you currently feel and behave. Rate yourself on a scale of 0 to 4.

0 = I NEVER feel or behave that way.
1 = I RARELY feel or behave that way (25% of the time).
2 = I SOMETIMES feel or behave that way (50% of the time).
3 - I USUALLY feel or behave that way (75% of the time).
4 = I ALWAYS feel or behave that way (100% of the time).

Score ... Self-Esteem Statements

___ 1. I accept myself the way I am right now.

___ 2. I am worthy, simply because I exist. I do not have to earn my worthiness.

___ 3. I get my needs met before I meet the needs of others.

___ 4. I do not let it get me down when other people blame or criticize me.

___ 5. I do not allow others to hurt me or put me down.

___ 6. I do not compare myself to other people.

___ 7. I feel equal to other people regardless of my performance, looks, I.Q., or achievements (or lack of).

___ 8. I take responsibility for my feelings and emotions. I do not blame others when I am upset, angry, or hurt.

___ 9. I learn from my mistakes rather than use them to confirm my unworthiness.

___ 10. I separate my behavior from the essence of who I am.

___ 11. I understand that I can choose to love each human being without having an active relationship with them.

___ 12. I accept other people as they are, even when they do not meet my expectations or I dislike their behavior.

____ 13. I am not responsible for anyone else's actions, needs, thoughts, moods, or feelings: only for my own.

____ 14. I feel my own feelings and think my own thoughts, even when those around me think or feel differently.

____ 15. I am kind to myself and do not use "shoulds" and "oughts" to put myself down with value-judging comments.

____ 16. I allow others to have their own interpretation and experience of me.

____ 17. I look for something positive in each individual I meet.

____ 18. I forgive myself and others for making mistakes and being unaware.

____ 19. I accept responsibility for my interpretation of other people's behavior and my responses to them.

____ 20. I do not dominate others or allow others to dominate me.

____ 21. I am my own authority. I make decisions that are for others' good and my own highest good.

____ 22. I develop and use my talents.

____ 23. I balance giving and receiving in my life.

___ 24. I am responsible for changing what I
       do not like in my life.
___ 25. I choose to love and respect every
       human being including myself.

Add up your score. It is a percentile
giving you feedback on your degree
of self-esteem (love of self). Place no
judgments as to what is a good score.
Use the questions where you assigned
a lower number as an indication of
where you might benefit from change.
Create affirmations (using positive
language) and visualizations of how
you want things to be to improve how
you feel.

Examples and more information are
given in *YOU COULD FEEL GOOD*, by
Suzanne E. Harrill.

About the Twelve Steps

I have rewritten the Twelve Steps of Alcoholics Anonymous for people working on the universal need to love and support themselves.

Many people who read the original Twelve Steps have a problem stating "I am powerless." Those people who practice reprogramming their subconscious mind through positive affirmation do not believe in stating a negative such as this.

I find it helpful to talk about the self in two parts: the little self (ego, conditioned self, or personality self) and the Greater Self (Spiritual Self, Transpersonal Self, or Higher Self). In reality there is no split; they are one. Until a person experiences this oneness, however, it seems as if there is a separation or split.

The Twelve Steps of Building Self-Esteem address this split. By practicing this process of healing through these Twelve Steps, one is capable of experiencing the truth which is wholeness.

The Twelve Steps move a person from the powerless state of consciousness of the little self to an empowered Spiritually Awakened Being. The personality self is created from the past and is subject to addiction, pain, illusion, and fear. The experiences of childhood conditioned the personality. Since most parenting was not totally adequate (no blame implied), the personality self is stuck wanting what it did not get in the past. This focus on the past of pain, deprivation, etc. creates the split from the Higher Self. The Twelve Steps help you on the spiritual journey of knowing who you are, a Spiritual Being having a physical experience.

The Twelve Steps of Building Self-Esteem

(Adapted from the Twelve Steps of Alcoholics Anonymous)

1. I admit my little self (ego) is powerless to control my negative thoughts and feelings—-my life of feeling unworthy is not working and is unmanageable.

2. I believe my wholeness depends on experiencing Love from God as I understand God (Higher Self, God Within).

3. I choose to turn my life over to the care and direction of my Higher Self (God Within) to become fully conscious, a self-actualized being.

4. I continue to know myself, looking at all past behavior, guiding beliefs, and feelings that have manifested negatively in my life.

5. I admit and forgive myself for fearful thoughts, words, and actions that block Love in my life.

6. I am ready to transform all aspects of myself that block the power of Love in my life.

7. I humbly ask my Higher Self (God Within) to achieve this transformation.

8. I make a list of all the situations and people whom I believe I have hurt or whom I feel have hurt me, because of unawareness. I am willing to make peace with my past.

9. I heal these relationships directly unless it does not support the highest good.

10. I continue to expand my awareness and heal negative patterns that I see. I admit my mistakes openly and take responsibility for my life.

11. I consciously experience more and more Love from my Higher Self through prayer, meditation, and contemplation. I chose to consciously express this Divine Love through me.

12. I am an awakening spiritual being as a result of practicing these steps. I continue to practice these principles and to love myself and others. I share this love with others who choose my assistance.

These Twelve Steps were rewritten by Suzanne E. Harrill, M.Ed., L.P.C. (713)661-8284

New Beginnings

It's a brand new year.
Today, I have a new beginning, a fresh
  new start.
I let go of yesterday's fears and take a
  step forward on my path.
As I focus on this present day, I choose
  to love and support myself.
I release old negative patterns, and I
  live fully in this day.
I find my way back to my life path if I
  have been diverted.
I commit to discovering and being
  exactly who I am.

I love the being that is me.

Potential Self

I am like an acorn growing into my Full-Potential Self.

At each place along my life path I am a perfect expression of this Self.

I am being exactly what I am capable of being at each moment; this is dependent upon my degree of awareness.

As I grow in awareness, I do better and better expressing the real me.

As it is never too late for the mighty oak tree to grow new branches, it is never too late for me to grow in confidence and security in being my true Self or to develop my interests and talents.

I am growing into my potential.

Worthiness

I cannot earn being worthy of love and
    acceptance.
It is my birthright.
Nothing I do, say, or think can change
    this truth.
I am a unique expression of the Higher
    Power.
I am worthy and of value regardless of
    whether I have accepted this or not.
Today, I choose to believe I am of
    value and am an important part of
    life.
Eventually, I will feel worthy.

I am worthy because I exist.

Self-Acceptance

To feel good about myself, it is
important to accept myself the way I am
right now.
If I put conditions on my self-
acceptance, I miss the opportunity
today to feel good.
Wanting something begins the creative
process.
I may want to improve my communication
skills, exercise more, finish school, get
married, or be farther along in creating a
life that I want.
Today is my place of power; I am learning
to love and accept myself and am
beginning to create the life I desire.

I accept myself right now, today.

Unconditional Love

I no longer expect anyone else to love me
unconditionally.

If I turn my power over to others by relying
on them for my good feelings, then I am
bounced around by their moods and
their ability to love.

When I turn within and connect with my
Inner Self, a direct link to the Higher
Power, I learn to love myself.

Today, when I feel lonely, unworthy,
separate from others, and in need of
love, I will turn inward and ask my Inner
Self for this love without conditions.

I remember the truth that I cannot earn
love, as it is already available as my
birthright.

I unconditionally love myself.

Nurturing

I look for ways to nurture myself.
I realize that the unmet dependency needs of my inner child require attention from me.
When I am filled with love, people are then attracted to my wholeness.
I visualize my inner child being filled with love and affection from my adult self.
I sit or walk in nature and become very still in order to feel my oneness with the earth, plants, trees, and sky.
I take time to listen and respond to my inner needs.

I do one thing today that nurtures me.

Responsibility

Only I have the power to create my life the
way I want it.
I do not blame or give credit to anyone for
who and what I am today.
Though people and events have interacted
with me and influenced me, today I
become a detective searching to
understand what motivates me to think,
feel, and act as I do.
I choose to work on my awareness and to
take the risks necessary that will change
my life and allow me to become more
and more an expression of my True Self.

I am responsible for my own life.

Authority

I take responsibility for my choices.
Not making a choice, I realize, is a choice.
I willingly pay the consequences, both
  good and bad, for these choices.
I know I am in the "school of life" and learn
  from everything I do.
I no longer turn my power over to others to
  make my choices because I now am
  aware that I pay the consequences of
  their choices for me.
By making my own choices and taking
  responsibility for them, I become my own
  authority.

I am my own authority.

Going Within

I go within to feel good. I no longer
    evaluate my self-worth on outer
    appearances.
My value is not dependent on my
    achievements (or lack of them), what
    others expect of me, my physical beauty,
    the color of my hair or skin, my car, or the
    cost of my clothing.
The outer me creatively expresses how I
    think and feel on the inside of me.
Eventually, my inner beauty will shine.

*I allow my outer self to be a reflection of
my inner beauty and light.*

Inner Self

I listen to my Inner Self.
To build sound self-esteem, I get in touch
with my inner needs today.
I know not to base my good feelings (or
bad ones) on outer appearances,
people, or circumstances.
I take a few moments, right now, to close
my eyes and go inward.
I go to my place of peace and ask what I
need today to feel more balanced in
order to take the next step in expanding
my awareness.
Do I need more activity or less?
Do I need to work on my physical,
emotional, mental, or spiritual well-being?

---

*I acknowledge and listen to the voice of
my Inner Self.*

Achieving

I let go of seeking approval and value
    through my achievements.
I now do things to express the creative
    power within me.
I let my achievements be a form of personal
    pleasure.
I accept the cycles of my life.
I am worthy even when I am just "being"
    and not accomplishing measurable
    things.
During these inward cycles, the seeds of
    new achievements are sprouting and
    taking root.

*I enjoy creative power by using it to
achieve what is within me.*

Comparison

Today, I choose not to compare myself with
   anyone else.
This builds my self-esteem.
There is no longer a race to win.
I am a winner whether someone is ahead of
   me or behind me on the journey of life.
No one is better than or less than I am.
I no longer need to concern myself with
   how much progress I am making by
   looking at others.
I have a special assignment that only I can
   fulfill and that is to be "Me."
I have my own internal time schedule.

I stop comparing myself to others.

Conscious Awareness

Today, I look at my awareness.
I want to consciously know the things that
    have been hidden from my view.
My awareness is everything that has
    brought me to this present moment —
    my genetic code, family patterns,
    behavioral tendencies, every experience
    that has ever happened to me, and
    everything I am taking in with my six
    senses.
As I look at myself, I discover more and
    more of what has been unconscious
    to me.

*I discover more and more who I am by
becoming consciously aware.*

Free-Will Choice

As I become more and more aware of my
   inner needs, wishes, and values as
   opposed to what other people want for
   me, I make wiser choices.
I have greater free-will choice when I know
   my Inner Self.
Today, I support myself by making choices
   from this place of power.

*I expand my understanding of myself so
I have greater free-will choice.*

Past Pain

I release the pain of my past.
I no longer allow a difficult childhood, a
    marriage, or a negative-feeling
    experience to cripple the present day.
I see with detachment what took place in
    my past.
In order not to repeat patterns, I remember
    what happened.
I allow any hidden emotions to surface so
    that I can grieve; then I focus my mind in
    the present and see what is good and
    what is working.

*I am healing the pain and fear from
my past.*

Emotional Reactions

I am becoming aware that my emotional
reactions are bigger than the people or
events that trigger these emotional
reactions.

I am usually reacting to a pattern built up in
my mind from many similar hurtful issues
from my past.

Today, I am aware of my emotional
reactions and ask myself questions such
as, "Is this a pattern?" or "Has this
response happened in me before?" or
"What were the circumstances?" or "Of
whom does this situation remind me?"

I choose to release myself from the
emotional pain of the past by seeing the
person or event as a trigger and not the
cause of my upset feelings.

I allow people and events to "trigger"
me in order to make peace with
the past.

Value-Judging

Today, I stop finding fault with myself and others.

Rather than criticize or judge, I pay attention whenever I think I "should" or "ought" to do something differently.

These value-judgments lower my self-esteem.

To become more aware, I ask myself, "What am I willing to do, or not do, in the future if this situation comes up again?"

Then I live with the consequences of this choice.

I stop value-judging myself and others.

Mistakes

I am okay when I make a mistake; that is
    how I learn and grow.
If I had known the outcome of a choice
    before I made it, then I would have had
    the awareness to choose differently.
When I go over and over what I judge as
    bad or wrong, I lower my self-esteem.
I forgive myself for an unwise choice.
I learn from all mistakes which is the purpose
    behind the experience.

---

*I am accepting of myself when I make
a mistake.*

Feelings

My feelings are not right or wrong.
They are simply an inner guidance system
giving me feedback on what my
reactions are to everything going on in
my daily experiences.
I am learning to put words to what I am
feeling.
Once I do this, I can use my mind to make
changes that will benefit me.
I listen to my feelings.

I accept and allow myself to feel.

Emotional Victim

Today, I give up being an emotional victim
by seeing the part I play in the drama.
I must turn inward to receive strength from
the Higher Power.
I begin by releasing unrealistic
expectations.
I accept people and events that I cannot
change.
I can only work on myself.
As I change, I no longer play my role as a
victim.

I give up being an emotional victim.

Behavior

I choose to understand my unwanted
    behavior.
Today, I look behind my behavior to what
    the causes are.
All behavior makes sense if I look at my
    needs and the choices I make to get
    them met.
Some of my needs are unconscious to me.
This is where I will focus to get some clarity
    on why I do things I do not consciously
    want to do.
I go within and ask my Inner Self for
    thoughts, pictures, or feelings that give
    me clues to this puzzle.
I am patient with the process of expanding
    my awareness.

*All my behavior makes sense, so I am
easy on myself.*

Forgiveness

I forgive myself for things I have said,
    thought, or done in the past that I do not
    like.
I remind myself that I only did what I could
    do at that place in time, with the level of
    understanding I had.
It no longer serves me to use today's
    awareness to judge yesterday's actions.
Today, I know I would do it differently.
I have learned from my choices, even
    though they might have seemed to be
    mistakes.

---

*I forgive myself for unaware things I
have said and done in the past.*

Giving

I fill myself today so that I can respond
    appropriately to the needs of others.
I stay conscious of what my needs are so
    that my boundaries are respected.
When I forget to work on myself, I give to
    others so that I will receive.
This is an inappropriate way to give.
Unattached giving requires me to be filled
    up and to give from my overflow.

*I fulfill my needs so that I can give
unconditionally to others.*

Awareness

My present level of awareness determines
what I am capable of doing at each
moment.
Therefore, I am always doing my best.
I need to go easy on myself and be
forgiving when I cannot do what I think I
should do.
This is especially difficult to understand if I
am not able to repeat a behavior or
level of achievement.
My best includes all aspects of myself—-
physical, emotional, mental, and spiritual.
When one part of me is out of balance, it
affects the rest of me.

*I am doing my best at each moment
with my present level of awareness.*

Blame

It serves no purpose for me to blame myself or another for anything.

Blaming myself lowers my self-esteem. I am, however, responsible for everything I say, think, and do.

I learn from all consequences.

The negative consequences teach me to make more aware choices.

Today, I notice when I have a habit of punishing myself through blame.

I release this pattern.

When blame comes up, I ask myself questions such as, "What expectations or demands did I have that were not met?" or "What can I learn from this situation that will enable me to have a different outcome next time?"

I stop blaming myself for undesirable actions, thoughts, and feelings.

Forgiveness

I release myself from anything or anyone
that I believe has hurt me.
I forgive people, situations, and myself for
being unaware and causing me pain.
When I am ready, I detach and see us all as
characters in a play acting out parts in a
script that was written at an unconscious
level of awareness.
I see that the victims, as well as the
victimizers, were trapped, not realizing
that they had conscious choices.
Today, I am more aware and choose to
forgive so I can move beyond this script.
If this is a new idea for me, I may need time
to get past my anger, denial, and/or grief.

---

*I forgive every person, including myself,
for being unaware and causing me pain.*

Preferences

Today, I work on my awareness of areas where I allow myself to be hurt and disappointed by having expectations that are too high.

When I demand a certain emotional outcome, this demand is an emotional addiction.

It helps me to have a preference for a certain outcome rather than an addiction.

Preferences are soft and flexible; demands are hard and rigid.

Preferences allow me to flow around what cannot be changed.

I turn my emotional demands into preferences.

Goals

Today, I will think about my goals.
I set realistic goals in the proper time frame
 for me.
I need to evaluate, prioritize, and adjust
 these goals periodically.
Standards set too low or too high lower my
 good feelings about myself.
I use only myself as the standard of
 measure.
As I grow and change, these goals may
 change.

*I set realistic goals and expectations
for myself.*

Thoughts and Feelings

Today, I work on identifying my feelings with
words.
Every feeling has a thought behind it.
These can be grouped into two main
categories: love and fear.
I am getting better and better at
recognizing my love thoughts and
allowing myself to feel them.
I also listen to my fear thoughts so that I will
be aware of them.
I pull unhealthy seed thoughts planted in
the garden of my consciousness.
I am responsible for replanting seed
thoughts based upon love.

*I plant loving thoughts in the garden of
my mind.*

Boundaries

I pay attention to my boundaries.
I notice when I feel uncomfortable during
   my interactions with others.
If I do feel uncomfortable, I will take care of
   myself by making changes that support
   me.
I may need to communicate to another or
   simply stay conscious so that I do not
   agree to anything that does not feel right
   to me.
It is okay to say "no."
Some experiences are not healthy for me.

I set appropriate boundaries for myself.

My Mother

I love and appreciate my mother.
I am grateful for the gift of life she gave me
and the sacrifices she made for me.
All that I learned being her child is a part of
me now.
I release and forgive all the judgments and
criticisms I have about wanting things to
have been different in my childhood.
My inner mother loves and nurtures me.

(This passage may be read on your
mother's birthday.)

I love and appreciate my mother.

Others' Approval

It is okay if some people do not like me.
As I become more and more my real Self, I
  become less dependent on the approval
  of others for my well-being.
Some people will never like me, and I
  accept this.
I choose to love myself.
The choices I make regarding my behavior,
  wants, and needs are no longer based
  on the approval of others.

*I let go of expecting everyone to like
and support me.*

Giving

Today I focus on unconditional giving.
First, I fill myself emotionally and get my
  needs met; then I can give without an
  expectation of a return.
I listen to my Inner Self to identify what I
  need.
I meet these needs first so that my giving
  comes from the good feeling I get when
  expressing kindness towards another.

*I give love to the degree that
I am filled up.*

Receiving

I allow myself to receive.
When another person gives me a
   compliment or does a kindness for me, I
   accept the gift.
It is no longer something to be made light
   of, but rather, to be enjoyed and
   appreciated.
Giving and receiving are different halves of
   a whole.
One without the other is incomplete.

I receive graciously.

Behavior

I continue to detach from feelings of
worthiness that are based on my
behavior.

I realize that my behavior is predictable as
that is how I learned to get my needs
met.

To change behavior that I do not like, I first
determine my needs and then I look at
healthy ways to get those needs met.

I may want to observe people who are able
to get their needs met in a positive way;
they can serve as role models for me.

Finally, I take risks to follow though with
these new choices until these choices
become automatic for me.

My behavior is how I get my needs met.
I look at my needs today.

Authentic Intentions

My intentions are more important than
  other peoples' perceptions of them.
Though some people may criticize even my
  best intentions, I choose to communicate
  as genuinely and authentically as I am
  able.
I always have the understanding and
  support of the Higher Power when my
  intentions are good.

*I communicate with an intention of
being authentic and genuine.*

Mirrors

Everyone is my mirror.
I would not see something in another if it
were not a part of me.
I remember that everyone is capable of
wise and unwise actions.
Instead of judging them as good or bad, I
seek to learn from everyone I meet.
I spend time with the people who reflect my
goodness, love, and beauty.

*I see reflections of aspects of myself in
other people because they are
my mirrors.*

Talents

I feel good about myself when I develop my
talents and abilities.

My talents may or may not be
achievements highly valued
by society.

My gifts may be playing the piano, writing,
taking care of plants, working with
animals, playing sports, or having the
patience to listen to others in need.

I go within and remember the things I like to
do and what excites me about life.

It is time again to focus on my talents and
gifts so I can express more of who and
what I am.

I choose to develop and use my talents.

Higher Self

I am an expression of my Higher Self.
There is much more to me than my
personality, behavior, and mind.
I am a spiritual being that exists beyond the
physical level of awareness.
As I grow in awareness, I learn more about
this Greater Self.
I am never alone.
A personal relationship with my Greater Self
builds my love and acceptance for all of
me.
My Higher Self is my Spritual Self.

I am an expression of my Higher Self.

Nourishment

The energy from Spirit is the only real source
of my strength and power.

Today, I fill myself with Love from my Higher
Self which is able to easily receive energy
from Spirit.

As I live this day, I imagine golden energy
from a ball of light above my head
pouring down into my physical form.

This energy flows in and around and
through me to nourish all the cells of my
body.

My emotional well-being is uplifted by this
nourishment from Spirit.

*I nourish myself with love and light
from my Higher Self.*

Purpose

I have a special purpose only I can fulfill.
No one else is exactly like I am, so only I can
fulfill the destiny of being me.
As I learn and grow in consciousness, I
become more and more aware of my
spiritual purpose.
I begin with listening to the real Self on the
inside of me and let that express through
my human self.

*I have the important role of learning to
become my Self.*

Higher Will

As I get to know my Inner Self, I receive
communication from the Higher Power.
I ask this Power what the higher will and
purpose is for me.
I do this through meditation, prayer, and
time spent thinking and pondering.
By first putting myself in a receiving mode, I
am open to receive communication
from Spirit which might come as a picture
or thoughts or, perhaps, I receive a
feeling and only sense my intuition at
work.

*I align myself with the
Higher Will and Purpose.*

School of Life

Today, I look at life as if it were a school.
I remember that I am here to learn and
  grow and to become fully aware of who
  and what I am.
The challenges that come my way are seen
  as part of the curriculum that I signed up
  for at the spiritual level of my being.
Rather than criticize, deny, or avoid my
  problems, I see them as opportunities for
  growth.

*I am in the school of life and learn from
every experience.*

Problems

I choose to see the problems in the drama
of my life as a chance to do things
differently.
When I do this, I see alternatives that are
not obvious.
As I gather information on the issue giving
me difficulty, I see that there are people
who have walked a similar path before
me who are available to be my
teachers.
My problems are no longer traps; they are a
means to become more aware.

*I open my mind and heart in order to
see my problems differently.*

Love

I choose to express love today.
I begin with myself.
I see myself from the eyes of my Full-
Potential Self.
I extend this love and appreciation of
myself from my Self to all others.
Today, I notice what I like about myself and
all others.

*I love and appreciate myself from the
place of Spirit.*

Question

I remember to question new ideas that I
   read in books or hear from others.
Before blindly putting them into my
   consciousness, I like to think about and
   see their practical application.
I can then reprogram my subconscious
   mind by changing unhealthy guiding
   beliefs (rules by which I live my life) for
   new ones.
I like to think about and prove the validity of
   new ideas.

*I question as I open my mind to new
points of view.*

Love vs. Like

Today, I am aware of the difference
   between loving and liking.
I can unconditionally love someone and
   not like their behavior.
My like or dislike of someone is an emotional
   response; unconditionally loving them is
   a mental decision.
Unconditional love does not dictate any
   behavior.
Sometimes the most loving thing for me to
   do is to say, "no."

I love everyone including the people
whose behavior I dislike.

Intellectualizing

Today, I notice when I am "in my head"
    and not participating in my life.
Once I have gathered information to help
    me solve my dilemmas in life, I act on
    that information.
Talking about and analyzing my problems
    are good to a point, however, my growth
    stops when I spend too much time
    intellectualizing.
I now begin taking risks to apply what
    I know.

To grow, I experience what I know.

Illness

I let go of judging myself and others when
    there is physical illness.
Illness does not mean a failure in spiritual
    growth.
I pay attention to the messages my body
    gives me in the metaphor of illness,
    aches, or pain.
As I crack the code of the metaphors, I
    make positive changes to heal my
    thoughts and feelings.
I also take care of myself on the physical
    level.

*I listen when my body talks to me
through illness and pain.*

Peace

World peace begins with me.
Today, I practice loving and forgiving so
that I can experience inner peace.
It is predictable that I will get my feelings
hurt or want to defend myself when
another pushes my emotional buttons.
In order to change my reactive behavior
and feelings, I balance myself by
choosing inner peace.
I do this by continually practicing thoughts
of love and forgiveness.

I choose inner peace.

Fear

Fear no longer stops my progress.
Today, I notice when I let my fear stop me
from taking risks.
If I visualize negative results when I see one
of my goals, I stop and bring my mind
back to the present moment.
When I use my mind appropriately, I see the
goal and determine the next step for me
in the process.
I talk gently and firmly to myself with my self-
talk by affirming my ability to risk even
when there is fear.

*I feel my fear and take positive risks
anyway.*

Assimilating

Many times I have judged myself as failing
to grow when I have reached a plateau.
Today, I remind myself that a lot takes place
on these plateaus.
I am assimilating what I have learned.
I am always growing.

I accept the plateaus in my life.

Value

I am of equal value to every other living being.
Talents, abilities, interests, energy levels, and awareness vary between people.
These things are not proof of my worthiness or unworthiness.
Comparison to others no longer determines my self-esteem.

I am of equal value and importance to every other person.

Approval

I become aware of my security needs that are dependent upon other people's approval.

As I learn new values, attitudes, beliefs, and behaviors, I do not expect others to always understand or be able to give me their approval.

It is important to allow others to disagree with me.

As I learn to love and support myself, I will not need approval or agreement from others to change my life.

I release the need for the approval of others in order to feel loved and supported as I change and grow.

Self-Talk

I monitor my self-talk.

When I hear criticism, "shoulds," and put downs, I override them with positive, encouraging, nonjudgmental words.

If I hear negative comments from others directed to me, I will not let this stick in my mind.

I will talk to them in person, if appropriate, or have a conversation with them in my mind as it is important to have the part of me that feels shut down and unworthy express my point of view.

I talk kindly to myself today.

Avoidance

Today, I pay attention to what makes me
uncomfortable.
I notice the things I want to avoid. I pay
attention to my body awareness and the
feelings that come up for me.
I choose to stay with my discomfort knowing
it is showing me something.
I then ponder the thoughts and feelings to
determine what I need to do with the
information, if anything.
Sometimes just being aware of what is
taking place is enough.

I face what makes me
feel uncomfortable.

Expectations

Today, I accept where I am in my growth.
I can expect too much from myself
    sometimes.
It no longer serves me to expect myself to
    be farther along the path of life.
I can only be where I am.
I build my self-esteem by knowing where I
    am going and knowing it takes time to
    put into practice what I have learned.

*I let go of expecting too much, too fast
from myself.*

Strength

Today I ask the Higher Power for strength.
As I become more and more aware of the
   places that I need to take risks in order to
   grow in a healthy direction, I choose to fill
   myself from Spirit.
My Higher Self receives radiant light energy
   from Spirit and adjusts it to the perfect
   frequency for me.
I imagine a shower of golden energy
   flowing in, around, and through me from
   a point above my head.

*I am strong because I fill myself with
energy from Spirit.*

Spiritual Arrogance

Today, I pay attention and respond in an
appropriate manner for my level of
spiritual awareness rather than acting as
if I were farther along my spiritual path
than I really am.
Spiritual arrogance can trick me if I am not
aware.
I realize where I am at this moment without
putting myself down or pumping myself
up.
Both are inappropriate for my growth.

*I practice being realistic by accepting
where I am in my spiritual growth.*

Magical Day

Today is a special bonus day.
I allow my inner secret wishes, hopes, and
    dreams to be known to myself.
I write them down in my journal so that I
    remember what they are.
As I become aware of what I want, this
    awareness plants seeds in the garden of
    my mind; they then become potential
    goals.
What I feel I want combined with what I see
    in my mind moves me in that direction.

---

*My path appears as I allow my wishes,
    hopes, and dreams to surface.*

Grounding

I work on grounding myself today.
I picture my feet planted firmly on the
    ground.
I see Mother Earth radiating energy up
    through the bottom of my feet,
    energizing me.
I feel the solid feeling of being in my
    physical body; I notice the boundary of
    my skin.
As I remember to connect to this solid
    place, I remain centered as I go through
    life's experiences.
It helps me think clearly and take care of
    myself.

*I ground myself with the support of
Mother Earth.*

Improving

Each time I see what another person could
    do to improve his or her life, I bring my
    attention back to myself.
I am the only person I can change; I have
    no control over others.
Each person can only act according to his
    or her level of awareness.
I have enough to work on to improve
    myself.

*I work only on changing myself;
changing others is not my responsibility.*

Teacher

Today, I remind myself that everyone is my
teacher.
I choose to learn from the people I dislike as
well as from those I like.
I pay attention to what my teachers are
mirroring for me today.
I would not see something in another unless
I also have it within me.
My power to express my goodness
increases as I see what I like and dislike
reflected by the teachers in my life.

*I see everyone as my teacher; they
reflect parts of myself.*

Blinders

Sometimes it is easy to wish I could go back to being less responsible for my life: that I could put up blinders and not see so much.

As I see parts of myself that I do not like, I continue to look.

In reality, I cannot put blinders up and go back to being unaware.

I can, however, choose to love and comfort myself.

I can take a break from the fast track of self-discovery.

A slower pace is nurturing sometimes.

*I slow the pace of self-discovery
when I get tired.*

One Day

I remind myself to live one day at a time.
When changes need to be made, it can be
  overwhelming.
It is appropriate to take risks and to set new
  goals, but thinking too much about the
  future robs me of my good feelings
  today.
I remember to live today and focus on only
  what is appropriate for my growth right
  now.

I live one day at a time.

Heart Opening

I ask for the courage to open my heart to
the love and support that is in my life.
I let it in.
Asking for help is a sign of strength and
humility.
I release the fears from the past that
impede my growth.
I trust the process of opening my heart to
experience love.

*I open my heart to receive
love and support.*

Inner Female

My female side knows how to love and
   nurture myself and others.
I turn inward today to listen to and to feel
   this wisdom.
Lessons in bonding with others are my
   curriculum today.
I notice when I put up emotional
   boundaries in relating to others.
I integrate the gentleness of my inner
   female into the greater me.

*I follow the guidance of my inner
female today.*

Inner Male

My inner male knows how to protect and
encourage me when I go out into the
world.
I listen to the wisdom of this part of my
consciousness today.
I notice situations when I do not take care
of and protect myself.
When I need help or encouragement, I will
draw on the strength of my inner male.

*I receive encouragement and protection
from my inner male.*

Journal

I write my thoughts, feelings, and insights in
   a journal.
I record my reactions to people and events,
   and I relate them to what my lessons for
   growth are during this passage of my life.
My pain, sadness, anger, hurts, and fears
   are eased as I write them down.
I receive clarity when I put what I feel into
   words.
I also write my feelings of joy,
   connectedness, comfort, and love.

*I keep a journal to help me grow and
integrate my inner feelings and reactions.*

Risks

I take a risk today that moves me out of a "stuck" pattern.

If I am unsure of what to do, I try something different.

Trial and error eventually will present something that works for me.

I hold something in my right hand, such as an acorn, to anchor me and remind me of my intention to break out of a "stuck" or crystallized pattern.

A small risk is just as important as a giant risk.

***I take risks to break out of unwanted
habits and patterns.***

Visualization

I think about what I want.

I can create only from the possibilities of
what I see in my mind.

As I focus on what I want by using my
creative power of visualization, I put
energy into creating.

I explore alternative realities with my mind in
order to see which ones I really want.

I add power to these pictures by affirming
and feeling the pictures as if they are a
current reality.

*I visualize what I want in order to
make positive changes.*

Information

I gather information today to make positive
    changes in my life.
I read or listen to tapes that serve my
    awareness.
Many teachers have put their ideas in
    books and/or tapes that can help me.
I take in information with an open mind
    using my thinking skills and body
    awareness to decide what is wise
    information for me to consider.
I notice if I feel good or bad after exposure
    to new teachings.
I also notice if I feel less confused or more
    confused.

*I listen to my Inner Self to determine
whether or not to follow a certain teacher.*

Time Alone

I spend at least half an hour today to think,
    ponder, daydream, journal write,
    meditate, or pray.
This time alone is a gift to myself to calm
    and center myself so I can make the
    changes in my life that I need to make.
I will spend this quality time with myself each
    and every day.

I spend time alone to think, to feel, and
to heal.

Healthy People

I spend time with people who reflect my
  inner beauty and love, people who are
  growing and working on improving
  themselves, and people who love
  themselves.
This helps me to make positive changes.
Their skills rub off on me which helps when I
  must work or live with unaware people.

*I spend time with healthy people who
reflect my wholeness.*

Hidden Meaning

I look for the meaning behind unwanted
   experiences.
This helps me grow.
I am like a detective investigating what part
   I play in these experiences so that I can
   stop repeating them.
When I see the "big picture," it helps me
   understand what is happening.
Then I can choose other behaviors, thinking
   patterns, or attitudes.

*I look for hidden meaning in my
experiences in order to grow
in consciousness.*

Courage

I have the courage to take another step
    towards fully loving myself.
I allow old feelings of devaluing myself to
    come to the surface.
After feeling them, I release them.
New feelings of lightness and aliveness flow
    into me.

*I ask for courage to release old feelings
of unworthiness and to fill myself with
feelings of warmth and tenderness.*

Confidence

I remember that from the acorn, a sapling
   has grown with its early branches barren
   and stunted.
It is time to grow those branches more fully.
One of them is confidence.
I am learning to feel confident as I gain
   comfort in being who I am on the inside.
I then take new risks to bring about
   balance and wholeness.

*I am growing confidence from within to
be exactly who I am.*

Trust

I trust the universe to support my growth into
my Full-Potential Self.
It matters not in what order I learn lessons to
be whole and complete .
At the end of my life, looking back, it will not
matter whether I trusted at birth or at
age forty or seventy-five.
It only matters that I learned to trust.

*I trust the process that I am unfolding
into my Full-Potential Self.*

Communion

I pay special attention to being connected
   to nature.
Moments of being in the silence of beauty
   enhances the blending of Spirit and
   matter.
A moment in the sunlight or rain with the
   breeze and plants, birds and animals stills
   my mind to feel the power behind such
   beauty.

*I commune with the Spirit in nature in
order to enhance the blend of Spirit
and matter within me.*

Pain

I listen to any pain I have inside of me
    whether it be physical, emotional,
    mental, or spiritual.
Pain easily talks to me and brings insight into
    the light.
As I understand and make changes, my
    pain leaves.
It has served its purpose which was to get
    my attention.

*As I listen to my pain, I hear the
messages guiding me to change.*

Being Right

I let go of needing to prove I am right.
It separates me from others who do not
    take my position.
Instead, I accept the fact that others may
    disagree with me and sometimes may
    not even want to know why I think or feel
    a certain way.
As I become secure in myself, I do not insist
    on being right.

*My good feelings about myself are not
determined by others' understanding or
agreeing with me.*

Deserving

I deserve love.

I release early teachings that led me to
    believe I was unworthy of love until I
    earned it.

I feel the warmth and love of my Higher Self
    pour down upon me healing the pain
    caused by the old beliefs.

I deserve and accept love in my life.

Inner Strength

I have the inner strength to meet the
  challenging experiences drawn into
  my life.
I remember to love and honor myself and
  to fill myself with healing energy from
  both the earth and Spirit.
As I center myself and feel solid in my
  physical form, I meet my day prepared.

*My inner strength carries me easily
through my challenges of the day.*

Alone

I set aside a special time to be alone with
    myself, away from the demands of the
    world.
I enjoy being with myself.
If any feelings of fear of loneliness present
    themselves to me, I remember I am
    never separate from my Higher Self.
I feel this connection with my Source as I
    experience the silence of being alone.

I enjoy being alone with myself.

Masks

I let go of the masks of who I think I should
be.
These masks served me from an earlier part
of my life; they were the only defenses I
knew how to use in order to survive.
My protection comes from the awareness I
now have.
I can still choose to wear a mask at times
when I know no other options.
This is temporary, however, because I am
learning day by day to be myself
regardless of other people's reactions to
me.

*I no longer need masks to hide my Inner
Self. I am enough all by myself.*

Power

I claim the power to be me.
I choose to express who I am on the inside.
I release comparing myself to other people.
I continue to discover the blueprint of my
    Full-Potential Self.
I release any parts of me acting through the
    mask of who I am not.
False expressions of me are no longer
    needed for my growth.
My inner beauty is ready to shine.

---

*I empower myself by being only
my True Self.*

Loving Kindness

I choose to live my life with loving kindness
even though I may appear to be soft
and vulnerable and easily hurt.
I, however, have a strength from within that
is able to set boundaries so others
cannot take advantage of me.
I choose these boundaries with awareness
and with an open heart that knows
loving kindness.
Sometimes the most kind and loving thing
to do is raise my voice or confront.
At other times, it is to remain silent and
remove myself from the drama.

*I choose to live my life with
loving kindness.*

Unhappiness

I feel unhappy when I am not honoring
   myself and have wandered off my life
   path.
As I learn to experience inner peace and
   live my life with awareness, I make
   choices that feel joyful.
I listen to the unhappy feelings so I can go
   within to find out what is needed for a
   correction.
Quiet time alone or with a special friend or
   spiritual teacher gives me the insight to
   make necessary changes.

*I listen to the messages my unhappy
feelings give me.*

Joy

Joy provides feedback that I am on track
    and that I am living from my soul.
As I learn to connect with my soul, I learn
    what my natural state is.
When I am in this place of soul connection, I
    easily go through the process of
    experiencing.
Even when things are difficult for my
    personality self (the physical, emotional,
    and mental sides of me), this soul
    connection allows me to connect with
    my Spiritual Self, and I can be joyful.
When I have spiritual awareness, I
    understand why I experience certain
    things.

*As I grow in my spiritual awareness,
I allow joy to radiate from within.*

Enjoyment

I pay attention to the things in life that give
me enjoyment.
Today, I choose to enjoy my day.
Even if something unexpected comes up
that throws me off center, I remember to
put things for enjoyment into my day.
One difficult moment does not ruin my
whole day.

I choose to enjoy my day.

The Journey

I allow my goals to guide me, and I remain
conscious of the process.
The journey is the real goal.
As soon as I achieve one goal, there is
always another and then another.
I find enjoyment in the journey.
Life is a process which I enter freely.
I accept the journey that is my life.

The journey of life is my ultimate goal.

Playfulness

I enter the day with the intention to play.
I look for ways to laugh as I celebrate April Fool's Day.
I really pay attention when a child or friend plays a joke on me. I let go of being serious; it is a day to be playful.
My inner child looks for simple ways to play and joke.

I let go and play.

Growth

I learn from everyone and everything that
    happens in my day.
As I make positive changes, I notice
    reactions both from within myself as well
    as from others.
I broaden my horizons when I pay attention
    to the times when I feel resistance from
    myself and others, as well as when I
    receive encouragement.
As I stay conscious, I receive insights into
    what maintains my growth and what
    stops my growth.

*Everything that comes my way is an
opportunity for my growth.*

Behavior

I am a spiritual being and am worthy even if
my behavior is bad.
I love and accept myself even when I do
not like my actions, habits, or
performance.
My self-esteem is no longer based on the
results of my behavior.
By separating my behavior from the spiritual
me, I know and feel my goodness.

I separate my behavior from the real me.

Growing

I am growing in many ways.
I notice the difference between my
   physical, emotional, mental, and spiritual
   needs.
I nurture the part of me that is in most need
   today.
The whole gestalt that I am benefits as this
   part of me is nurtured and is able to
   grow.

*I feed myself physically, emotionally,
mentally, and spiritually in order to
grow in a positive way.*

Perfect Order

At each stage in my growth and
   development, I am perfect being who I
   am.
I am doing only what I am capable of
   doing at each stage based on my
   awareness.
I honor the process of perfection unfolding
   in my consciousness.

*Each stage of my life unfolds in
perfect order.*

Life Challenges

Life challenges open my eyes to
   unconscious aspects of myself.
Without resistance and challenge, I would
   not notice or pay attention.
I grow as I experience a life challenge.
Though I may not sail through the passage
   of a life challenge, I remain aware in
   order to grow in consciousness.
I keep my spiritual eyes open to grow in
   conscious awareness of Self.

*I accept my life challenges as
opportunities for my growth and
awareness.*

Genuine Encounters

I am genuine in all my interactions with
others.
Only I can know for sure if I have a genuine
intention.
I am sincere and honest with myself and let
go of false pretenses.
I choose to relate from the heart of my true
Self.

*I am learning to be genuine in all my
relationships with others.*

Inner Vision

I do not judge anything I see today.
Instead, I look behind the circumstances of
my life for greater meaning and purpose.
I expand my inner vision to see what is really
going on.
I look for patterns that repeat themselves
rather than see myself as the effect of
these circumstances.
I see the patterns that are healthy and
those that are unhealthy and need
changing.

*My inner vision shows me what is
really going on behind circumstances.*

Evolution

I see my life evolving into greater meaning
and purpose.
Everything I think, feel, and do gives me
experiences to explore the meaning of
my life.
Today, I notice the unity of all life and feel
my place in it.
I spend time appreciating some aspect of
nature which connects me to this greater
unity.

*I accept the process of evolution.
My life has purpose and meaning.*

Self-Esteem

I am part of the greater universe.
My little self is part of my Greater Self.
I accept this connection and allow love
    from the Greater Self to nourish my little
    personality self which still gets caught up
    in the drama of life.
When I forget to love myself, I tune into this
    greater love coming from Self.

I reveive love from my Greater Self.

Importance of My Life

My life is important and counts.
I do not receive more or less value than
 anyone else.
It is important that I be who and what I am.
My life matters, and I make a difference. I
 am alive and, therefore, have a reason
 for being.
I allow the purpose of my life to unfold.

My life is important.
I make a difference.

Perfection

Today, I look at the perfection of my life
  which includes all the imperfections.
I am like that oak tree growing into greater
  degrees of maturity, perfect at each
  stage of growth.
I accept each stage of my growth and
  development without judgment.

*I am perfect at each stage of
my development.*

Challenges

I acknowledge and respond to my life
   challenges as they occur.
Avoiding them or denying them keeps me
   unaware.
As I do not like the surprise of hidden
   challenges that pop up when I least
   expect them, I gather information and
   take the risks necessary to meet these
   challenges and transform them.
This keeps me from repeating them which
   causes me unnecessary pain.

*I accept responsibility for transforming
my life challenges.*

Knowing Self

I am the person I spend the most time with so it is important to know myself inside and out.

It is not selfish to spend time knowing who I am, what my thoughts and beliefs are, and what my feelings are.

When I know myself, I avoid being manipulated by others or by life's circumstances.

I prepare myself by knowing myself well.

*I spend time
getting to know myself.*

Openness

I practice being open with myself and
   others today.
I use my intuition to give me feedback on
   how open to be.
I notice when others can match my
   openness and when they cannot.
I avoid setting myself up to be victimized by
   staying conscious while I am open to
   others less open to me.
My protection is my awareness.

*Staying consciously aware, I am open
with myself and others.*

Listening and Talking

In communicating with others, I balance my
    listening with my talking.
If either is lacking, I miss a chance to learn
    and grow in my relationships.
Both listening and talking are necessary in
    healthy relating.
It is important to really listen, not just remain
    silent, when relating to others.
It is also important to talk so that others can
    begin to understand me.

I balance my listening and talking
with others.

Consequences as Teachers

I allow myself to say, think, and do whatever
I choose without judging my value by the
outcome.

All of my thoughts, words, and actions have
consequences.

Some consequences will teach me to
repeat beliefs, words, and behaviors
while others will teach me that I do not
choose to repeat them.

*I pay attention to consequences.
However, I no longer judge my value
based on these consequences.*

Patterns

I choose to see the patterns of my life.
Painful patterns from my early conditioning
surface so that I can release feelings of
powerlessness.
Once I see a pattern repeating, (the
people may be different but the
circumstances are similar), I then have
the free will to do something differently.

*My past patterns no longer control me.
I see them and make new choices.*

Repressed Feelings

I allow feelings to surface as I am ready to process them.

Sometimes my freedom to enjoy the present is stopped by repressed feelings.

I surround myself with love, and I breathe deeply and ask myself to bring forward a situation from the past that is not resolved, understood, or even conscious.

I close my eyes and scan the years of my life.

As I choose a time period, I patiently choose one incident to work on.

As feelings come up, I may need to cry or hit a pillow.

I journal write and then go for a walk to feel the healing power of nature.

I seek outside help when I need additional support.

I allow repressed feelings to surface in order to transform them into the light of understanding and forgiveness.

Emotional Reactions

I notice the emotional outbursts and strong
   reactions I have today.
They are clues to the unconscious issues
   that I have to resolve.
When I am alone, I take the time to ask
   myself how the current person or situation
   is part of a greater pattern.
As I do this, I find it easier and easier to
   forgive the current situation and to have
   a healthy response based on current
   feelings and reactions.

*I am learning to respond with wisdom
rather than overreact to
people and events.*

Asking

I ask for what I need and want; then I let go
and allow the universe to respond.
If another person is involved, I receive what
they are capable of giving.
I am open to new or different ways of
getting my wants and needs met.
Sometimes I have to wait for proper timing
or until after I remove my blocks to
receiving.

*I let my needs and wants be known and
allow them to be met, sometimes, in
unexpected ways.*

Looking Beyond Duality

I accept that there is meaning in everything
    that happens to me.
I look behind judgments of good and bad
    to see what the hidden aspects are in
    situations that are difficult for me to
    accept.
I look for a third option whenever I am
    caught in an "either/or" situation.

*I look for meaningful choices of
thoughts, words, and actions that move
me beyond duality thinking of
"either/or."*

Excitement

I look for what ignites my interest in life.
This feeling gives me feedback on what is
    stimulating to me.
I pay attention to my inner needs to
    determine whether I need more or less
    excitement in my day.
It is important to find some excitement in
    each day to enjoy living.

*I am excited about my day. This
excitement gives joy to my life.*

The Psychic Buck

I pay attention to where I need to take
  responsibility for my life.
I no longer pass the psychic buck to
  someone else.
For example, I may have the power to have
  most of the world agreeing that I am a
  victim.
This may give me sympathy; however, it
  stops my growth and keeps me stuck in
  the victim pattern.
I no longer pass this responsibility on to
  another.

*I accept responsibility for my life. The
  psychic buck stops here.*

Enmeshment

I disentangle myself from enmeshment in
  other peoples' boundaries.
I notice when I lose a sense of self and am
  caught up in other peoples' dramas.
I stop being the one to make everyone feel
  better at the expense of taking care of
  myself.

*I am clear with my boundaries to avoid
enmeshment into other peoples'
problems and emotional reactions.*

Balance

I pay attention to my needs and wants
observing how they affect the people
around me.
I have the desire to balance my needs with
other people's needs.
When in conflict, I determine, to the best of
my ability, who has the greater need at
the time so that person (whether it's me
or not) can receive first.
I choose not to dominate or be dominated.
The balance of give and take is important in
my close relationships.

*I balance my needs with the
needs of others.*

Right Action

I tune into my Inner Self to determine what is
    right for me to do in each situation I
    experience in life.

When unclear, I go to a quiet place to think,
    then I am able to see beyond emotional
    and defensive reactions.

No one can tell me what I should do; they
    can only tell me what they might do in
    my situation.

I get clear with myself on what my motives
    are for any action; so that right action will
    follow.

I allow right action to flow through me.

Wise Use of Power

I pay attention today to how I use my
    power.
I notice if I feel powerless or powerful.
I empower myself with kindness and love so
    that I can use my power wisely.
If I dominate and force my will over another,
    I notice this and make amends.
In learning to use my power wisely, I may
    make mistakes and experience extremes
    sometimes.
Staying conscious makes me able to make
    corrections.

I use my power wisely.

Loving Kindness

I live my life from a position of love.
I am clear that coming from an intention of
    love does not dictate any specific
    behavior.
Sometimes the most loving thing to do is to
    remove myself from a situation or to
    confront another.
All I need do is focus on this intention to
    come from loving kindness and to
    practice it on myself as well as on others.

*I live my life from the place of
loving kindness.*

Encouragement

I give myself encouragement to move
 forward on healing myself.
I talk gently, but firmly, to myself as I move
 forward on my journey.
I take the risks to change my unwanted
 patterns of thinking and behaving even
 though it may feel unfamiliar and
 uncomfortable.
I know I can change; I can keep going.

*I encourage myself to take another step
forward in healing myself, my
relationships, and the earth.*

Honoring Myself

I honor myself today.
I respect and appreciate the beauty and
    perfection of who I am.
I treat myself with the love and respect that
    I show to others.
It is a privilege to be who I am as I learn and
    grow in consciousness.

I honor myself with the respect, love,
and reverence of a Sacred Being.

Trusting Intuition

My only real protection in life is being able
to trust my intuition.

As I learn to trust my intuition, I become
aware that I am safe.

Situations and people are perceived by my
five senses — sight, hearing, touch, taste,
and smell.

These senses are not always enough to give
me information to make wise choices.

My intuition gives me the missing
information.

My intuition can help me discover life-
purpose choices or more basic survival-
level choices such as who to trust (by
feeling and knowing when someone's
intentions are incongruent with their
actions) or when a dangerous situation is
to be avoided.

My intuition allows me to stop depending
on other people to take care of me.

*I listen to my inner guidance. My
intuition guides and protects me.*

Evaluating Self

I stop evaluating my worth by measuring
  myself against my expectations.
It is good to have standards and to be
  aware of my values.
Today I take stock of how I think I am doing
  in living my values and standards.
I may need to list my values to become
  more aware of them.
I eliminate any that say I should value
  something based on someone else's
  value system (unless I feel it is "right" for
  me).
I notice progress I have made; small steps
  are important.
If I have feelings of failure, I use them for
  motivation and begin again to meet my
  internal standards.

*I evaluate myself today to see my
progress. I feel good when I live by my
values and standards.*

Power to Choose

I have the power to choose my thoughts
and behavior.
I can improve how I feel by either changing
my thoughts or my behavior.
I choose one thought or one behavior to
work on today.
I will see myself improving this thought or
behavior.
Every time I begin to think or act in the old
way, I will gently refocus on the new idea
I'm learning.

*I have the power to feel better by
choosing better thoughts or behaviors.
I visualize the new thought or behavior
over and over to help me live it.*

Body Awareness

I focus on relaxing my body today.

I take deep breaths to use more of my lung capacity which calms me and lessens my stress level.

I pull myself up by an imaginary string at the top of my head which is connected to the top of my spine.

I allow my arms to hang loose.

I balance on my feet and allow the ankle bone, knee, hip, shoulder, and ear to align.

I move my arms and torso when I walk.

I live comfortably in my body. By deep breathing and aligning my skeletal system, I receive the support I need.

Focus

I pay attention to where I am going.
I focus on what I want to accomplish today.
I begin by performing simple tasks such as
    making my bed or making a phone call.
I step towards meeting a hidden desire.
When I focus on what I want, I know which
    direction to take even when all the steps
    are not clear.

***I focus on what I want so I can move in
that direction.***

Emotional Strength

I am emotionally strong.
I know that no matter what other people
 say or do to me, they cannot take away
 my awareness that I am a worthwhile
 person.
My inner life is mine and nothing can take
 away my realization of my innate worth.

*I am a worthwhile person no matter
what others say or do to me.*

Daily Goals

I like to know what I will do with my day.
I write a list of goals I wish to accomplish
  each morning.
My list of goals includes time to think and
  work on myself.
I respond to my physical and emotional
  cycles.
Sometimes I move quicker than at other
  times.
It nurtures me to manage my time.

I set daily goals to use my time wisely.

Making a Difference

My life counts in the grand scheme of
    things.
I make a difference.
I am to be me, and no one else can take
    my place.
I allow my inner feelings to guide me on
    where I can use my talents to make a
    better world.
I begin with thinking good thoughts about
    myself, and I pursue possibilities of getting
    involved where I can contribute.

I make a difference; my life counts.

My Body

I take care of my body.
Connecting spiritually, attuning to my
    intuition, and connecting with my Higher
    Self are easier when my body is running
    smoothly.
I work from where my body is presently, not
    comparing myself to other people or to
    me in the past.
I eat foods that promote my good health.
I exercise and get proper rest.

*My body is my friend, and I
take care of it.*

Helping Others

I like to help others.
I get my own needs met so that I have
    energy to give to others.
Service performed from my overflow of
    energy balances me.
I pay attention to what others' needs are,
    which may be different from making
    things "nice" for them or doing what they
    may need to be doing for themselves.

I like to help others. I serve from a
place of balancing my needs with
others' needs.

Love

I remember who I am. I am Love.
I am a worthy part of the Universe.
I am okay, and I deserve to take care of
    myself, get my needs met, and create
    what I want.
This simple message is the most important
    step in my journey.

I am Love.

Authority of My Soul

Eventually, I have to listen to my soul and comply with what the spiritual agenda is for me.

This takes courage, a willingness to break out of old patterns, and a willingness to keep growing in order to heal my early conditioning.

When I listen, my life really gets easier.

I find my way through the rough passages and share the wisdom I have gained with others.

I listen to the authority of my soul.

Curiosity

I am curious about everything around me.
I learn more and more about myself when I
   pay attention and question people,
   events, feelings, thoughts, reactions, etc.
   in my environment.
It is good to use my curiosity; it takes me into
   realms of greater understanding.

---

*I learn about myself by being curious
about everything in my environment.*

Open-Mindedness

I open my mind to new ideas outside of my
   present belief system.
Rather than disagree or put down a new
   idea, I consider the possibility of its truth.
I gather more information about the idea
   before deciding whether or not it is of
   value to me.
I observe people who believe this new way
   in order to determine if they are
   expressing incongruities or if they have
   an inner peace about them.

*I have a free and open mind to explore
new ideas.*

Contribution

As I feel better and better about myself, I
  have the ability to contribute to those
  around me and to the greater service of
  humanity.
I want to give back what I receive in order
  to keep the cycle of giving and receiving
  flowing.
I automatically give by being in a positive
  state of mind as I grow into greater and
  greater awareness.
It is just as important to give a smile and to
  reply kindly to the grocery checker as it is
  to join the Peace Corps or to run my
  business with the bottom line of human
  kindness; all make a contribution to the
  healing of the world.

*I make a contribution to the world by
first learning to feel good about myself
and then passing human kindness
on to others.*

Shame

I release my feelings of shame.
I detach myself from being embarrassed
    about having needs.
Everyone has needs.
My inner child has needs, and I am here to
    comfort and support my inner child.
The adults who raised me or taught me
    could only pass on to me reflections of
    their level of consciousness.
Today, I recognize their lack of awareness in
    the shame that was passed on to me.
I am good, and it is okay to have needs
    and to be needy at times.
I no longer have to be ashamed of these
    needs.

*I release feelings of shame; no one is to
blame. I am free to feel my feelings,
even the needy dependent ones.*

Motivation

I am motivated to improve my life.
I first see in my mind's eye the probabilities
    that will benefit me.
Once I can see a future action that excites
    me and benefits me, I am automatically
    motivated.
The more I go within to determine what is
    right for me, the more my inner urges and
    pictures emerge to guide and motivate
    me.

***Once I see the way to go, I easily
motivate myself.***

Real Needs

I go within to get in touch with my real
   needs.
I may have been conditioned by outer
   needs for success, popularity, and
   achievement coming from parents,
   teachers, peers, T.V., etc.
I may have missed a whole set of inner
   needs: ones that come from within me.
These are my real needs.
Wise motivation comes from getting to
   these real needs.

*I go within to discover my real needs as
they provide the motivation to create
my life in the perfect way for me.*

My Shadow

I pay attention to traits in others that I do not like.

Whatever I disown in myself shows up in other people.

By owning my shadow or dark side (those parts of myself that I do not like and have made unconscious to myself), I take responsibility for my life.

I am capable of all actions, thoughts, and feelings, good as well as evil.

Rather than judge or be victimized by people with certain traits, I acknowledge that they are hidden parts of me.

I get to choose what to act on from my shadow side when it is made conscious.

I lose my power of choice when I project it onto another person and call them bad or evil.

I allow my shadow to come into my awareness at the pace I can handle. I empower myself by owning this side of me.

Well-Being

I allow myself to feel good.
I get a sense of well-being by accepting
    that I am good and doing the best that I
    can at each moment with my level of
    awareness.
I no longer compare myself to anyone.
I am growing in consciousness at the
    perfect pace for me.
I accept inner peace by choosing to feel
    good and by having a strong, positive
    sense of well-being.

*My sense of well-being gives me inner
peace and strength to go forward.*

Weighing Consequences

I make choices today by looking at the
   probable outcomes.
I weigh the consequences of each choice
   to determine the wisest choice for me.
If I am willing to pay the consequences,
   then I am free to make any choice.
I take responsibility for my choices, both
   wise and unwise.

*I make wise choices by weighing
consequences before I choose.*

Free Will

I look at my free will to make choices.

If I am aware of my true needs, then I can use my free will to make choices that support my highest good and my understanding of myself.

If I am on the fence between two choices, I work on expanding my awareness of my Inner Self.

The awareness of my inner needs helps me take the risks involved in exercising my free will.

Others will make choices for me if I do not.

Not making a choice also is a choice.

I accept the privilege of having free will. I use my free will to make conscious choices.

Gentle Strength

I use my gentle strength to move forward today.

I take note of situations when I need to confront and make a change.

I overcome the fear of using my power to get what I want or need.

If I feel overpowered by something or someone, I may need to use my power to get results.

I use my gentle side at the same time in order not to overcorrect.

(Sometimes I go from one extreme of feeling powerless and victimized to the other extreme of feeling powerful and victimizing).

The in-between place of knowing my limits, boundaries, and desires and, at the same time, being flexible and responsive are called forth with gentle strength.

I use my gentle strength when I need to confront and make a change.

Inner Freedom

I am free because I am growing and
getting to know myself.

I understand why I do many things which
gives me the power of using my free will
to improve my life and solve my
problems.

My inner freedom allows me to watch
myself in my interactions with others and
to disengage from the drama.

When I see how and why I got to this
moment, I have incredible inner
freedom.

I am free because I have inner freedom.

Humility

I acknowledge myself for who and what
and why I am.
This gives me the opportunity to live my life
with humility.
I no longer have the need to have every
good deed or accomplishment
acknowledged by others.
I take private joy in living my life with quiet
humility.

*I am humble because I no longer have
the need to prove myself.*

Value-Judging

I stop value-judging others and let them live by their own code of values.

I am secure in my values.

I have no need to impose my values on others who do not agree with me.

I allow others to have their value system without judgment from me.

I notice when I make others wrong in my mind.

This gives me the opportunity to fine tune my release of value-judging.

I choose to live my life free of validating myself based on whether or not other people agree with me.

I am secure in my value system and no longer need agreement from others to feel good.

Physical Health

I take care of my physical self.
No matter how good my intentions are to
    take risks or to emotionally feel good, I
    can only do so to the degree that my
    physical body is balanced and well.
I take care of any imbalances in diet,
    exercise, or sleep.
I get help from professionals if necessary.

*I improve my physical health. My
strong physical mechanism allows
more Spirit to operate through me.*

Strengths

I list my strengths and the things I can do.
I need to remind myself often of my full
    potential for goodness and higher
    consciousness.
When I express myself from this set of
    strengths, I meet my challenges better.
I then motivate myself to express my talents,
    connect to others, and feel good about
    myself.

*I see and appreciate my strengths. I am
proud of the things I can do.*

Memorial Day

I pay tribute to others who died in wars.
I forgive the consciousness in those times for
    using physical violence to settle power
    struggles which was the only way
    humanity at that time knew how to settle
    conflicts with other countries.
I am grateful to be alive today when this
    consciousness is in the process of
    changing.
I do my part to eliminate the power of war
    to exist on the planet by solving my
    personal power struggles through
    communication, love, and empowering
    my opponents.
When each of us feels safe, loved, and
    powerful, the world will no longer need
    to use physical force or authoritarianism
    to settle disputes.

I solve my power struggles in
nonviolent ways.

Survival

I am okay, and I know I am capable of
 surviving.
I have up to this point.
I am able to find my way when I stray from
 my path.
I can find answers within, as well as outside,
 myself.
I have the power now to attract people,
 information, and experiences that help
 me face my shadow or unconscious
 parts of myself.
When I illuminate with understanding what
 scares me, I find only light.

*I am a survivor and able to transform
my unconscious into conscious
awareness.*

Recovery

I am recovering from the illusions of my
conditioned past and early childhood.
I am strong now that I have the tools to
speed my recovery.
Energy that was blocked because of living
from the illusion of fear, pain, and
separation from my Spiritual Self is now
available.
I am learning to create my life from this
place of wholeness.

*I rejoice in the process of recovery that
has helped me awaken.*

New Ideas

I plant new ideas or seed thoughts in my
    mind.

I focus on inspirational ideas that suggest
    the direction of healing and wholeness
    for me.

A simple test to let me know this positive
    direction is to ask myself whether a
    certain teaching makes me feel good,
    connected to my Self, or whether it
    makes me feel fearful, shameful, and
    disconnected from my Self.

When I was one, two, and three years old, I
    trusted this ability to guide me.

I return to this inner guidance system so I
    can plant healthy seed thoughts in my
    consciousness.

---

*I plant new ideas in my mind that
inspire me to grow and change in the
direction of my highest good.*

Nourishment

I fertilize and water new seed thoughts in my mind so they will grow and serve me to live my life from my Full-Potential Self.

I repeat these seed thoughts over and over until they become a part of my new belief system.

I reinforce these new ideas by reading, taking classes, and being around other people who support and reflect these ideas.

I give myself nourishment to help new seed thoughts grow and blossom.

Integration

I listen to the inner parts of myself.
Those parts that have conflict and pain
    need to learn blending and integration
    into the greater whole of me.
I listen to competing and immature aspects
    of myself so they will feel understood.
I love these parts of myself so they will feel
    safe to mature and will want to
    cooperate on the same team.
I need to integrate all aspects of myself to
    feel whole.
All parts of me have a positive intention
    somewhere.
Once I learn their positive intention, I can
    appreciate and call forth this energy as
    needed on the conscious level.

*I allow all parts of me to be heard so I
can blend and integrate their energy
into the service of my Higher Self.*

Organization

I organize my life on all levels.
I begin with the mundane by cleaning out
   my closets, drawers, files, and the trunk of
   my car.
I release items that no longer serve me.
If I do not use or like clothing or possessions,
   I give them away.
I next look at how I use my time.
I give myself permission to eliminate
   spending time doing things that do not
   support my growth or highest good.
I balance my time between doing and
   being.

I organize my possessions and time.

Life-Style Changes

I take a mental inventory today, noticing areas of my life in which I need a permanent change of habit.

I make a list of the new behaviors desired and I use them as goals.

A life-style change is a process that takes time and energy.

I give myself this needed time and forgive myself when I am not able to maintain new behaviors.

I read this list of goals often to impact my subconscious mind.

The more I feel a strong desire for this life-style change, the faster I create it.

I desire permanent life-style changes that support my new level of awareness.

Resistance

I notice when I resist people, ideas,
    suggestions, or inner wisdom.
I slow down and listen to my fears as they
    need to be expressed.
I honor my resistances as they show me
    where I need to spend time looking at
    unconscious blocks.
I can only progress as fast as my resistances
    will allow.

I learn from what I resist.

Spiritual Guidance

I ask for spiritual guidance to help me over
the rough spots.
The answers may come from direct
experience with the Source, in a book,
from T.V., or from another person.
I am receptive to help when it answers my
call for guidance.

*I receive help whenever I ask for
spiritual guidance.*

Humor

I allow myself to see humor in my life.
When I take myself too seriously, I miss
    enjoying the moment by being "in my
    head," practicing being right.
As I lighten up, I use laughter to make it
    through many of the rough spots.
I notice feelings are expressed and tension
    released when I laugh at myself.

I stop taking myself so seriously.
I laugh at myself.

Opening Communication

I open communication with those people I
    care about.
I openly express myself and talk about my
    feelings and experiences.
I let go of expectations of the other person.
I listen and do not offer suggestions unless
    asked.
I listen "between the lines" to get the real
    message the other person is sending and
    respond to this rather than the exact
    words.
I pay attention to nonverbal
    communication such as body language
    and tone of voice.

*I feel connected to loved ones when I
use open communication skills.*

Inner Resistance

I pay attention to my inner resistances to
    others.
This tension may be felt in my body even if
    my mind is able to rationalize and justify
    my position or point of view.
As I release this inner resistance, I heal my
    outer relationships with people.
Sometimes the healing of the relationship
    requires that I remove myself from the
    relationship, at least for a time, if it seems
    that the situation will not change.

*I let go of my inner resistance to
other people.*

Courage

I have the courage to take another step
towards fully loving myself.

As old feelings of devaluing myself arise, I
allow them to surface.

I feel them and then let them go, cleansing
my emotional body.

I imagine lying on the shore line at the edge
of the beach, allowing the waves to
wash over me.

As I feel the water subside, I imagine the old
feelings dissolving into the ocean.

I stand up with courage to face my future
empty and waiting for the new to
blossom from within me.

***I have the courage to move forward
after emotionally cleansing my
consciousness.***

Confidence

I am confident and comfortable in being
who I am.
As I trust in the perfection of who I am, I
more easily take risks to grow into my
wholeness.
I am perfect at each stage of my growth.

*I deserve to feel confident and self-
assured as I grow into my True Self.*

Trust

I trust the universe to bring me the perfect
    experience to support my growth into my
    Full-Potential Self.
I trust myself to perceive what is going on in
    relating with people and events.
Rather than trusting others to support me, I
    take responsibility to listen to my intuition.

*I trust my feelings, perceptions, and
intuition to take care of me.*

Communion

I connect to the outdoors today.
I choose one thing to relate to, such as a
    tree, or a squirrel or a leaf or a cloud.
I allow a part of myself to exchange energy
    with this magnificent part of nature.

*I enjoy communion with the Spirit
in nature .*

Body Pain

I listen to my pain so that I receive the
  communication my body is sending.
I pay attention to where the pain is
  registering in my body.
The body sends messages, even if I am
  unaware of hurting emotions and
  conflicting beliefs.
When I pay attention, I use the pain as
  information that something is "off," and I
  go within to discover the problem.
I thank my body for being such a sensitive
  instrument registering conflict and calling
  attention to changes I need to make.

*I am in rapport with my body. I listen
to my feelings to receive my
body's messages.*

Weeding the Garden

I take inventory today of all the things in my
life that I no longer want in the garden of
my life.

Seeds that were planted in less aware days
that are not in alignment with my present
consciousness need to be removed or
transplanted to where they are needed.

I look at my current surroundings and give
away what is no longer needed.

I do the same with guiding beliefs,
outmoded ideas, and thoughts that stop
my growth.

*I weed the garden of my life so new
seed thoughts can grow.*

Cause and Effect

I pay attention to the law of cause and
   effect operating in my life.
I take note of what I like that is being
   experienced.
I look behind this effect to see how I
   created what is now happening.
As I expand this ability to see, I can repeat
   what I like.
More and more, I am able to cause my life
   to be the way I want it to be.

*I am empowered to be the cause in my
life. I remember always to tune into my
Higher Self.*

Playing My Hand

I play the hand I am dealt each day to the
best of my ability.
Though some things appear to be
challenging my ability to change, I
expand my awareness in order to
participate in the game of life.
I watch myself as I go through the
challenging experiences.
Being the observer allows me to see that I
can make changes.

*I am good at playing the hand I am
dealt each day.*

My Best

My self-worth is not dependent on how well
    I live each day.
I am worthy because I am part of the
    Greater Whole living in physical
    expression.
I do the best I can to figure out the game
    called life.
As I live each day, I give it my best and pick
    myself up if I stumble.

*I keep going; I am doing my best
each day.*

Summer Solstice

I align myself to the greater order and
  rhythm of the earth.
I feel this year's day of greatest light.
Today, I read and ponder the significance
  of the Great Invocation written by Alice
  Bailey in 1936. (See the next page.)

---

*I align myself with the Greater Rhythm
of life's cycles.*

The Great Invocation

From the point of Light within the Mind of God
    Let light stream forth into the minds
        of men.
    Let Light descend on Earth.

From the point of Love within the Heart of God
    Let love stream forth into the
        hearts of men.
    May Christ return to Earth.

From the centre where the Will of God is known
    Let purpose guide the little wills of men -
    The purpose which the Masters
        know and serve.

From the centre which we call the race of men
    Let the Plan of Love and Light work out
    And may it seal the door where
        evil dwells.

Let Light and Love and Power restore the
    Plan on Earth.

This Invocation or Prayer does not belong to any person or group, but to all Humanity. The beauty and the strength of this Invocation lies in its simplicity, and in its expression of certain central truths which all men, innately and normally, accept - the truth of the existence of a basic Intelligence to Whom we vaguely give the name of God; the truth that behind all outer seeming, the motivating power of the universe is Love; the truth that a great Individuality came to earth, called by Christians, the Christ, and embodied that love so that we could understand; the truth that both love and intelligence are effects of what is called the Will of God; and finally the self-evident truth that only through *humanity* itself can the Divine Plan work out.

Alice A. Bailey,
in her book *From Bethlehem to Calvary*

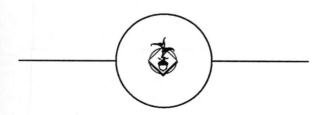

Joy

I take joy in this moment and in this day.
I sometimes hurt in the process of being
    who I am and disengaging from what is
    dysfunctional.
I remain joyful from the level of my soul
    knowing that I have found the way.
I can change my conditioned past so that I
    am a whole, fully-functioning adult.

*I am joyful because I have found my
way home to wholeness.*

Conflicts

I spend time alone to process my conflicts
with other people.

I no longer suppress or deny my feelings as
they come up during or after a
confrontation.

I look behind the conflict to see what my
part is.

I ask myself questions such as, "What would
I do differently?", "What did I not see that
caught me off guard?", "What patterns
am I working on?", etc.

If I feel it would be beneficial, I talk it over
later with the other person.

*I process my thoughts and feelings after
experiencing conflict with another.*

Inner Child

I nurture my inner child today.
I pay attention to hidden dependency
    needs that I project onto others.
When I catch myself feeling low because
    another cannot hold or touch or listen, I
    remember to nurture my inner child.
I may close my eyes and picture myself at
    an early age and bring this part of me
    that needs nurturing to sit on the lap of
    my present self.
As I hold this child and love this child,
    she/he talks to me, and I listen.
I express my love and show the way to
    wholeness, sharing all that I have learned
    so the pain does not have to be
    reexperienced.

I spend time nurturing my inner child
whenever I feel
others have let me down.

Inner Work

I spend time doing inner work on myself so that I can steer my life out of pain and confusion.

I listen to my feelings and thoughts today in order to take my inner temperature.

This lets me know what I need to do today to fill myself.

If I need to be touched and no one else is available, I may schedule a massage or spend time with animals.

If I need to move my body, I may walk or exercise.

If I need stimulation for my mind, I may buy a new book or take a class or go to a lecture to feed my intellectual hunger.

If I feel disconnected from people, I may find a support group to join or a workshop to take or go to counseling.

I spend time doing the inner work necessary to solve my problems and fill myself.

Religious Guilt

I release guilt that is a result of breaking the rules of religious dogma.

I now have permission to question, explore, and decide how I wish to connect with the Source.

Though I respect religious traditions, I look at the symbolism behind the rituals and ceremonies.

I allow the Higher Love, Will, and Power to come into my life in ways that agree with my particular personality.

It is no longer important how I worship the Higher Power; it is only important that I do.

*I am loved, honored, and respected by
the Source of all creation
and I return this.*

History

My history does not need to predict the
    future.
As I learn who I am, what my needs are,
    and how to expand my awareness, I look
    at the matrix of patterns that were
    formed in my family of origin.
As I notice the negative patterns, I look at
    how they were acted out or how I
    overcorrected and acted out the
    opposite.
I know that my power to move beyond the
    crystallization of these past negative
    patterns is in the moment.
I do not need to repeat these patterns
    because I am willing to look at my history
    and to remember it.

*I am aware of my history so I can
correct, in the present, any negativity I
do not choose to take with me
into the future.*

Active Intelligence

I use my mind before I take action.
To break out of unneeded patterns, I must
  think before I act or speak.
My mind, used at its best, steers my
  consciousness to greater freedom,
  awareness, and wholeness.
I spend time thinking about what I need to
  do to grow into greater wholeness.
My intellect is my friend, and I think before
  taking action.

*I use active intelligence to bridge
between what I need to do and what I
am doing.*

Comfort

I seek nurturing and comfort when I find it
    necessary to change the pattern of
    acting out early negative patterns.
I do the work of self-healing by relying on
    my support systems.
I gladly accept the guidance of a teacher,
    mentor, or counselor to help me on this
    new path.
Without the maps and the wayshowers, I
    would randomly stumble along.
I receive comfort from those who show me
    the way.
I see that they can do it, and I know that I
    can also.

*I feel great comfort because I have
found people to show me the way.*

Dislikes

I learn from my dislikes.
What I do not like is the only internal
    feedback I have sometimes.
I use this information to help me discover
    what I do like and value.
I stop using my dislikes to complain or stay
    stuck or to criticize either myself or others.
I pay attention to what makes me
    uncomfortable, brings up criticism, or
    plays "poor me" self-talk.
I ponder to discover what my dislikes are
    really telling me about what I want to
    create and experience and enjoy.

*I pay attention to and learn from what
I do not like. My dislikes give me clues
to what I really want.*

Depression

I listen to my inner needs when my emotions feel heavy, low, and out of sorts.

I spend quality time with myself when I am "down" emotionally.

I remember what anchors me and helps me get in touch with why I am feeling depressed.

I may receive nurturing from music, flowers, being in nature, being with animals or a pet, a cherished item from childhood, or a crystal, to name just a few.

As I tune into my Inner Self, I determine what needs attention.

I seek help from others if I cannot do this alone.

I listen to the feedback my Inner Self is giving me when I feel depressed.

Maintenance

I take care of my physical body and my
   material possessions.
I notice what needs to be fixed in my home
   (this means the physical space I live in).
I make a plan to take care of what is
   needing repair.
I may need a physical examination, to
   recover a chair, or to throw out
   unneeded items and clothing.
I spend the day paying attention to
   maintaining my physical world.

**I maintain my physical body
and possessions.**

Roadblocks

I make a list of the roadblocks in my
   consciousness that need leveling.
When I get in my own way, I stop my growth
   and awareness process.
By seeing the blocks, I know that my
   immediate agenda is to heal myself.
I create affirmations to move past these
   roadblocks.
For example, if I neglect spending time on
   my self growth, I may want to often say
   things such as, "I am worth an investment
   of time and energy," or "I choose to
   spend time learning why I do not like to
   take care of myself," or "I commit to
   reading five pages a day from a book
   that has information to help me solve my
   problems."

I face the roadblocks to my progress.
I create affirmations to know and
help myself.

The Land of Opportunity

I celebrate this land of opportunity.
I am grateful to live in a land with the
theme of personal freedom and
opportunity because I am free to live my
life the way I choose.
I meet this responsibility by becoming the
best I can be.
I choose to live up to this responsibility by
monitoring my actions, thoughts, and
feelings.
I wish this land of opportunity to continue in
freedom and peace for all its people.

I live my life to express my Full-
Potential Self, which is my part to
perpetuate this land of opportunity.

A Lighted House

I create a home and body that is full of
  light.
When I am infused with the Light of Spirit, I
  can light the way for others who are a
  step behind me on the path.
I allow the light to shine in all the dark
  corners of my physical home and
  physical body.
I release what is old and not needed as
  they collect dust in my closets and my
  consciousness.

*I build a life in a lighted house: a place
of refuge and comfort for
myself and others.*

Soul-Infused Personality

I watch as the dominance of my personality
    wanes and the authority of my soul
    waxes.
I am in the process of becoming a soul-
    infused personality living from the place
    of spiritual goodwill.
I need the personality as long as I am living
    in a body in order to blend it with the
    energy of my soul.

I am a personality that is spiritually
motivated by the will of my soul .

Path

The labyrinth was a diversion.
I leave behind the running around, as I now
  know that I was lost and afraid to admit it.
I am no longer confused looking for, but not
  finding, the exit.
The goal is my own healing which will allow
  me to unify with the greater whole.
I am back on the path, and it feels good to
  be home.
I am in the process of awakening to all I am
  meant to be.

I am joyful to be on the path.

Secret

Wholeness is my secret.

I do not expect anyone to understand or notice my journey into wholeness and the integration of my many parts.

I release the need for those who are close to me to understand where I am in consciousness.

If I still need to share, I do so only with those who are consciously working on themselves.

I do not burden others who are not yet on the path of awareness by sharing too much of my spiritual journey.

My journey into wholeness is my secret.
It is not necessary for me
to have others notice.

Negative Thoughts

I pay attention to the thoughts I have about myself today.

I listen to the voice in my mind, paying strict attention to the negative thoughts.

I talk back to the negative self-talk telling it the new truths I am learning about my innate worthiness.

I ask people close to me, especially people in my family, what they believe are my negative thoughts about myself.

Usually the critical, negative, or judgmental things I say to others when I am upset gives me clues to what I am really saying to myself.

Once I discover this negative mind talk, I turn it around into positive, healthy affirmations and guiding beliefs.

I say kind, loving, and nurturing things to myself.

Loving Relationships

I have loving relationships to the degree that I have a loving relationship with myself.

Today, I begin improving my relationships by working on myself.

I communicate my needs and wants and listen to the people I love and care about.

I practice unconditional acceptance of myself and the people in my life.

I send warm and loving thoughts to my partner, children, parents, siblings, friends, neighbors, and co-workers.

I take the time to work on improving relationships with those with whom I am in conflict.

I feel warm and loving towards all the people in my life.

Staying Present

I stay present in today's experiences.
I concern myself only with what I need to
    do today.
If I can do something today to effect
    tomorrow, then I do it.
Otherwise, I stop worrying about tomorrow.
If I redo and relive the past, I stop and
    remind myself to live in the present, the
    here and now.
I release myself from focusing on the past
    by remembering I need to forgive—-
    again and again if necessary.

I concern myself with the present.
This is enough to keep me busy.

Power

I am powerful because I am part of the
    creative Godforce and accept the
    assignment of creating my life.
I do this with joy and understanding. I am in
    charge of creating what I do with my life.
It feels good to be a powerful creator.

I am powerful.

Tolerance

I practice being tolerant today.
When people do not behave to my liking, I
 will be tolerant of them.
I will look behind their behavior to see why
 they do and say the things they do, then
 I will think through how I want to handle
 the situation.
I will change my reactions by being
 tolerant.
If I am being harmed and/or violated, I will
 remove myself from the situation.

I am tolerant of others today.

Limitations

I look at the boundaries of what I see as
limitations in my life.
I explore to see if they are still valid.
I release outdated restrictions.
I look to the doorway to find a way out of
my current limitations.
I walk through this threshold and enter a
universe of unlimited potential.
I seek greater expansion.

*I release my limitations and walk
through the doorway of unlimited
potential. I am ready to expand
my horizons.*

Success

I accept every experience as part of the success of living my life.

If I have experiences that do not support my growth, I remember that they teach me choices that I do not want to make again.

Every day, I do better and better at living my life with a feeling of success.

I made it this far, and I have learned that being willing to take risks provides me with greater and greater successes.

I know my life is a success.

Shame

I give up being ashamed.
I let go of any thoughts, feelings, or actions
    that I feel are a mistake.
I no longer give fuel to this old feeling I
    learned in early life.
If I make a mistake, I am not bad.
If I have emotional dependency needs, I
    acknowledge them and do not hide
    from these needs.
I can only heal what I am aware of.
I fill my inner child that feels devalued with
    love and golden light.
I allow my grown-up self to nurture this inner
    child.

*I am proud to be me. I heal the parts of
me that do not feel whole and complete.*

Learning

I make a list of things I want to learn to do.
It does not matter how old I am or what my
   physical limitations are.
If I am interested in developing a skill or
   experiencing something, I put it on
   the list.
I begin planning and daydreaming about
   where to start.
I will read this list of things I want to learn
   whenever I am bored.
This could be a perfect time to learn new
   things.

Today I begin learning one new thing.

Roles

I make a list in my journal of all the roles I
  play.
I evaluate how these roles are supporting
  me.
Do I need to change some or renegotiate
  others?
I go within today to plan how to eliminate
  the roles that no longer serve me.
If I negatively affect people close to me, I
  begin talking to them about my
  awareness of my roles and what I might
  want to change.

I play my roles consciously.

Synchronisity

I look back at the series of coincidences
that have shaped my life.
I see the synchronisity (one or more events
which seem to be chance at first notice,
but in fact, are of great significance).
These events brought me to today even
though they went unnoticed at the time
they occurred.
I allow the universe to continue subtly
directing my live with synchronisity.

*I allow the wisdom of the universe to
direct my life. I notice the synchronisity
of events as I live my day.*

Angel of the Universe

I am an angel of the universe. Wherever I
go, the creative Source of all things is
with me as me.
The presence of oneness surrounds me as I
jump off with folded wings.
Then, my wings unfold as I trust and feel the
safety of my loving and supportive God.
The exultation of the flight of freedom is
here to meet my fear of flying.

*I am an angel of the universe freely
soaring through the dimensions
with freedom.*

Flying

I am up here having made the jump,
   proving that my spirit can fly.
As I look back, I see how this was the only
   path I could take.
To the right and left and above and below,
   I find new companions; they have been
   waiting for me to ascend.
In front of me are those ready to guide and
   show me the way.

*I feel joy from taking the risk to fly
with Spirit. I am doing it now!*

Ahead on the Path

Ahead of me I see light and openness
   which is full of unrealized potential, the
   material to create my future.
The raw materials are here in abundance.
I have earned this freedom of creation by
   jumping off with my angel wings into this
   uncharted territory in consciousness.

*Ahead of me on the path, I see the light
of creative substance that is available
to me. I move toward greater and
greater potential.*

Time

I have the time to do the things I want to
   do.
If I am pressured with too many things to do,
   I have a serious talk with myself today to
   determine what needs to be released.
If I am bored and spend too much time
   alone being passive, I also have a serious
   talk with myself about being willing to
   take risks and adding activity in my life.
I balance my time wisely between doing
   and being.

*I use my time wisely so I have time to
do the things I want to do.*

Remembering

I remember who I am.
I am a spiritual being living in the school called Earth.
I am part of the Source of all things.
When I experience pain, fear, or anxiety, I soothe my little self by remembering who I really am.
My higher consciousness takes over when I remember, and I calm down and relax into knowing who I am.

I remember that I am an important part of the Universe.

Light on the Path

The Light of Spirit illuminates my path.
I do not have to see the whole picture as I
trust the Light to guide me to the next
step.
As I turn around to review my life, I see the
plan clearly and realize that it is a better
plan than my personality self could have
created.
I take each step trusting my Higher Self to
guide me in the appropriate destination.

The light is on my path showing me the
next step to take. I take this step with
trust and anticipation.

I Am

I am a part of the universe and that makes
my life important.
The individual piece of consciousness that I
am is transformed daily as I expand my
awareness of myself and of life.
Each day I am a greater expression of my
Self.
I am the Source expressing in a physical,
emotional, mental, and spiritual unit
called ME.

*I am a conscious piece of the Universe,
growing and expressing as me.*

Children

I notice children today.
They help me remember the full potential in
  myself.
If I have my own children, I feel
  appreciation for them.
I remember the privilege it is to be their
  parent.
I express the love and gratitude I feel to my
  children.

*I love the children in my life. I express
my gratitude to them today.*

Living Love

I take one day at a time and live it to the
　　fullest.
This is living my purpose.
Even if I understand the greater significance
　　of my life, I can only live today's purpose.
Today, I tune into why I am really here: to
　　extend love, to be loved.

**_I am one who leads the way in
living love._**

Present Moment

I no longer believe in coincidences in my
  life.
Everything that I have experienced has
  been important to bring me to this point
  in time.
I continue to put together the puzzle of who
  I am, so I can make sense of my life and
  see the purpose and plan behind outer
  appearances.

*Everything I have experienced has
purposefully led me to
this present moment.*

The Unconscious

I accept the unconscious part of my being.

We experience duality here on Earth. Light and shadow exist as opposites of the same thing.

As I expand my conscious awareness, I shine the light of awareness into the unconscious part of my being.

This transforms my fear of the darkness and unknown into the light of understanding and awareness.

As I progress on my spiritual journey, I grow into the light.

I accept the parts of me that are unconscious. As I shine the light of awareness into the shadow part of me, I transcend my fear .

Spiritual Teachers

I pay attention to how information
resonates within me to know if a teacher
is right for me.

Teachers can come in the form of authors,
therapists, ministers, gurus, and friends.

If I feel free and closer to knowing my true
Self, then a teacher is good for me.

I evaluate my reactions, body feelings, and
thoughts when I am with a teacher.

This takes me closer to God and wholeness.

*I attract a teacher that resonates
with me.*

Anger

I stop fearing other people's anger.
My inner child may feel scared and want to
    take responsibility when another person
    erupts, but the adult within me is strong
    now and able to talk to and soothe the
    fear of my inner child.
I see angry people as being in pain and
    scapegoating responsibility for their pain.
I detach from taking responsibility for other
    people's anger.
I own my own anger and process it without
    blaming and hurting others.

*I take responsibility for feeling only
my own anger .*

My Body

I am worthy of having a beautiful physical
    form and presence.
My thoughts direct my body.
I pay attention to mixed messages I send
    my body.
I give it clear, loving, reasonable, and
    achievable directions.
My body wants to please me.
My body knows how to balance itself and
    communicates with me when it needs
    something such as exercise or stretching
    or fasting.
I listen when my body talks.

I love my body and my body loves me.

Food

I thank my food for nourishing and building
my body.
My body is in charge of directing the food.
If I should eat something I believe is bad
and will, for example, make me fat, then
I change my thinking.
My body knows how to turn up the
thermostat to metabolize excess food if I
believe this is so.

*Food is my friend. I bless the food that
I eat and let my body process it for my
highest good.*

Opening

I open my heart today to feel all the good
   in my life.

I am the gatekeeper and can close the
   gate, if I choose, in situations that are
   beyond my ability.

Eventually, I will open to all and not be
   susceptible to being hurt or angered by
   other people and situations.

Today, I appreciate what is good and
   loving in my life.

I open the gate to my heart to this love and
   goodness.

*I open my heart to love and support in
my life.*

Compassion

I am connected to all people everywhere.
I have loving compassion for all the people
of the world.
I send love to others who I do not know
personally, so they will progress on their
journey in this life.
Suffering or undergoing life's challenges is
made easier with the loving compassion
of others.
I have a kind thought, word, or action for all
the people in my life today.
I extend my love by having compassion for
people today.

*I live my life with loving compassion
for all others.*

Animals

I appreciate the animal kingdom.
I learn a lot about myself by watching
   animals.
I communicate with an animal today in
   order to experience the blending of my
   consciousness with another living being.
As I observe a pet, a bird, or squirrel, I
   imagine what they are thinking and
   feeling.
It comforts me to spend time being with
   animals.

*I experience communion with an
animal to learn about myself and
exchange love.*

Wholeness

I remember to see my wholeness rather
than to dwell on the challenges that a
part of me experiences.
I center myself continually.
I release the importance of the drama in
my life.
The main focus of my day is my wholeness.

I am whole and complete right now.

Plants

I love and appreciate the beauty that
   plants bring to my life.
They nurture and soothe me when I am
   stressed.
A walk among greenery calms and
   balances me.
I practice extending my consciousness to a
   plant or tree in order to feel its
   consciousness.

*I spend time with plants and trees and
flowers to balance my emotions and
blend consciousness.*

Sunlight

I receive the energy of the sun today.
I spend a few moments in sunlight to
experience the full spectrum of light,
which is necessary for my health.
I appreciate the process of photosynthesis
which allows me to consume the energy
of the sun in the form of plants I eat and
to breathe in energy from the air.
My life is made possible from the energy of
the sun.

*I live in gratitude for the light the sun
shines on me.*

Balance

I live my life with balance.
I pay attention to any part of me that needs
help whether it be physical, emotional,
mental, or spiritual.
I correct anything that does not support my
balance.
I notice what keeps me in alignment and
remember to make these things a habit
in my life.

*I balance myself physically,
emotionally, mentally, and spiritually.*

Peace

I create inner peace in my life.
I focus on meeting my inner needs so I can
   enjoy peace in my outer world.
Peaceful thoughts and words to myself
   dissolve my conflicts.
As I meet others, I silently greet them by
   affirming, "Peace be with you."
For at least a moment, they feel my energy
   as a mirror of calm peace.

*I live from the place of peace within me
   and reflect it to all others I meet.*

Color

I use color in my environment and clothing
   to influence my emotional body.
I notice the colors that balance me and
   help me change patterns and habits.
If, for example, I easily scatter my energy
   and move too quickly, I am expressing
   warm colors of reds and oranges and
   yellows.
Being around cool colors of blues, greens,
   and violets would help me create a
   balance.

*I am like an artist painting with a full
palette of colors in my life.*

Giving

I choose to give my energy where it is
    needed.
I allow myself to recognize the difference
    between people who need nurturing
    from me and those who refuse to learn to
    nurture themselves.
Those who need to learn self-nurturance
    benefit from my encouragement and
    not from my doing it for them.
I teach self-nurturing by modeling it and not
    by creating dependency.
If I choose to get involved with those who
    are "using" me, then I need to establish a
    fair exchange of energy.
I may, for example, charge for my services.

I give nurturing freely to those in need;
I remember to recognize
unhealthy dependency.

Assignment

I am a part of the Greater Whole; I am a
   necessary cell in the larger body called
   God or the Universe.
Without me, the Universe would not be
   complete.
I accept the assignment to be uniquely me.
I love and accept myself right now, this
   moment, and choose to complete my
   mission.

I accept my mission to be uniquely me.

Reawakening

I am reawakening to who I already am.
I no longer allow the early conditioning of
  my childhood to hold me back from the
  awareness of my goodness.
I willingly cooperate to express more and
  more the innate goodness that is within
  me.
I accept the process of pain, struggle, and
  disappointment to quicken within me the
  light of understanding.
I release all feelings of unworthiness.

*I reawaken to the awareness that I am
a part of God in physical expression.*

Vessel

My body is a vessel for Spirit.
It is my privilege to be a channel for the
    love and light of Spirit to use my talents
    and gifts in service of goodwill.
It is a great opportunity to be alive at this
    dynamic period in time and to know that
    I am a living unit of God.
I thank each cell in my body for living its
    purpose in order to give me a physical
    vehicle to be used as a perfect vessel for
    Spirit.

*I am a perfect vessel for the Higher
Will of Spirit to use in service to
humanity.*

Healing Relationships

It is time to be friends and to drop the
facade of not caring and not trusting.
I choose to make peace and drop the
script that makes another the "bad guy."
I release my resentments from the past.
I accept and support others to be who they
are and to do what they need to do.
I choose to see others' good qualities.
May the peace of understanding come to
each of us as we forgive ourselves and
each other.

I face the future as a friend to all.

Critical Mass

I am more conscious than unconscious
   now.
The inner battle is over as the critical mass
   for consciousness and light has been
   reached.
Life is much easier now.
I continue to heal any dark places in my
   consciousness that hook me into
   unhealthy attachment.
I march to the beat of the rhythm of my
   own soul now.

*The critical mass has been reached;
I live from the Light of my Soul.*

Relating with Feeling

My conflicts with others dissipate as I relate
   on a feeling level.
I hear the feelings behind others' words. I
   notice body language.
My power increases as I slow my reactions,
   and I stop telling, advising, and trying to
   fix others.
Instead, I allow others to drink from the oasis
   of my cool, clear, refreshing water of
   consciousness as I relate on a feeling
   level.

I relate on a feeling level with others.

Inner Vision

In order to see with my inner eyes, I release my judgments.
I let go of the polarity of beauty and harshness.
I see them as complimentary and not as opposites.
The inner vision I had as a child returns to me now.
I concern myself with living in the Now; I do not look too far into the future or rehash the past.
I have the patience to see the beauty of each experience.

My inner vision returns as I concern myself with the process of now; I let go of judgments and develop patience.

Adventure

Life is an adventure, and I explore
 uncharted territory.
Today, I choose an area to explore that is
 outside of my normal boundaries.
I may explore something on the physical
 level such as, walking in the wilderness or
 signing up for a karate class.
I may explore emotionally by joining a
 support group or taking a class on
 psychodrama, or I can explore mentally
 by reading a book outside my usual area
 of interest or belief system.
I can be a pioneer in consciousness by
 meditating.

*I see my life as an adventure with more
 and more to explore and experience.*

Spontaneity

I listen to my inner child today and live with
spontaneity.

Rather than get bogged down with my
lessons in self-discipline and responsibility,
I choose to be more spontaneous.

Those sudden moments that allow me to
exchange a smile with a salesperson or a
janitor or a child or a passerby are
enjoyed.

The brief connections of the heart are felt
everywhere I go today.

I lighten up and live with spontaneity.

Excitement

I allow myself to feel excited today.
Somewhere within me I know what is joyful
   to experience or express.
I can anticipate my new life unfolding when
   I live in a state of expanded
   consciousness.
I am excited about my new awareness
   even when I have challenges.
I am excited to discover how to live in the
   world and not get caught in the illusions
   or problems of the world.

*I am excited about my life and choose
to live from expanded consciousness.*

Enlightenment

I am in the process of "lightening" my
    consciousness.
I see that I go through doorways that bring
    me more and more understanding.
I experience a certain degree of
    enlightenment right now.
I trust the process of the Universe and know I
    will progress towards total enlightenment
    when the lessons are learned.
I share the light that I now possess with
    others.

---

*The journey of enlightenment is
progressing well in my life.*

My Rights

I have the right to complain, to return purchases to stores, or to write letters to managers when I do not receive proper goods or services.

When I pay for something, I have the right to have things work.

I can assert myself without being aggressive and hurtful.

I communicate openly and honestly to handle corrections in goods and services not correctly provided.

I assert myself when my rights are violated. I know I can take care of myself and receive what I pay for.

Loving Myself

I am responsible for loving myself.
I do not expect others to meet my needs.
I enjoy it when another can give me love,
    attention, and support.
When I become dependent on another
    and expect them to do for me what I
    cannot do for myself, I set myself up for
    disappointment.
I always return to the source of my being to
    love and care for myself.
I practice healing meditations with my inner
    child when I become too needy.
This reparenting by the Inner Self helps me
    to love myself in my day-to-day living.

I take responsibility for loving myself.

Looking Within

I look within to find my True Self.
My Spiritual Self reveals itself more and more
　　as I learn to go within in meditation,
　　contemplation, and journal writing.
As I question my reasons for acting a certain
　　way and my reasons for everything I do, I
　　am learning to tell the difference
　　between my conditioned personality
　　and my True Self.
It feels good to get to know and express my
　　True Self.

I look within to find my True Self.

Enough

I am enough by myself.
I do not need other people to make me
    whole.
I continue to work on loving myself
    completely.
As I learn to fill myself with love, I have no
    missing pieces that are dependent on
    other people to fulfill.
I am joyful knowing I can handle whatever
    may challenge my security today
    because I know that I am strong within.

*I am enough because I know how to
love myself.*

Inner Guidance

I listen to my inner guidance; it continually
    shows me the way out of the maze of
    illusion.

I spend enough time with myself to learn
    the difference between the control of
    the little self and wisdom of the Higher
    Self.

My inner wisdom can guide me better than
    I ever thought possible.

I see the goodness I experience when I
    release my outer drama and accept my
    inner guidance.

I listen to my inner guidance.

Power

I have the power to create my life the way I
    want.
The source of my power is my Spiritual Self
    which is linked to God.
I align my personality self with my Spiritual
    Self, and the energy flows easily.
I am clear in my mind what I want to
    create.
I visualize and affirm it, and then I allow the
    Universe to draw it to me.
I can create whatever I am able to accept.

*I accept the power to create what serves
my highest good.*

My Father

I honor the man who is or was my father in
life.
He played an important role for my life
script.
I send him love and peace to help him
grow further on his journey.
I release any residue of anger or hurt for
unmet expectations.
I internalize from this man the qualities I
need for my inner father.
Any missing qualities I need, I create myself.

(This passage may be read on
your father's birthday.)

I am a good father to my inner child.

Earth

I honor the earth and all she provides.
This unique planet loves and supports me.
I, in turn, take care of her.
I express gratitude for living on such a
    beautiful planet where I may see colors,
    trees, flowers, animals, water, mountains,
    and clouds.

I love the Earth and the Earth loves me.

Grounding

I feel the energy of the earth support me.
I stand with my feet in contact with the
  ground and visualize energy coming up
  from the earth.
This energy connects me in a solid way with
  this physical dimension.
I easily move around in my body.
I live safely and consciously.

*My feet ground me to the earth which
supports me in this world.*

Judgments from Others

Today, I detach from the judgments of
   others.
I make my own decisions based on the
   consequences I am willing to live with.
I no longer need an outside authority to tell
   me what to do.
I continue to detach from other peoples'
   criticism, expectations, and judgments of
   me.

*I detach from other peoples'
judgments of me.
I am my own authority.*

Diet

I pay attention to my diet; I eat foods that are full of life force and that enlighten my body.

I eat only food that is prepared in an atmosphere of love.

I bless my food before I eat it, to purify it for my body.

I give my gratitude to the plant and/or animal that is serving me.

I only eat when it is calm and peaceful.

I drink plenty of water.

When I am ready to make dietary changes, I begin gathering information about nutrition.

I love and nurture my body with high vibration foods, prepared and eaten in an atmosphere of love.

Exercise

I keep my body in good physical shape through yoga, movement, or an exercise program.

I walk and use stairs whenever possible in order to use my physical form.

If my body is "differently abled," I create a special program for me to get maximum strength from my body.

I create a strong physical form for Spirit to live in.

My body is a vehicle for my Spiritual Self to use.

I take care of my physical body with regular exercise designed for my needs.

Acceptance

I accept, not only myself, but other people
   as well.
Each of us is doing the best we can with our
   level of awareness.
Acceptance does not mean I have to be
   around someone who hurts me because
   they are unaware.
It is simply understanding them with
   compassion.

---

*I accept everyone wherever they are in
their level of awareness.*

Birthday

Today is my special day.

I give thanks to the people who gave birth to me.

I commit to loving myself from this day forward.

As I look in the mirror today, I say supportive, kind things to myself. I listen to my Inner Self.

I celebrate my day and am not dependent on others to make it my special day.

I treat myself to small, nurturing gifts.

(Exchange this passage with your birthday.)

I celebrate myself today.

Traits

My traits are neutral; they become positive or negative depending upon how I use them.

I make a list of my traits and use neutral words to describe them.

All negative traits have a positive compliment.

For example, my trait of codependency is the ability to respond to others with the intention of helping them.

I choose to get in touch with the positive use of my traits.

*I accept my unique set of personality
traits. They are me, and
I express them positively.*

Service

I dedicate my life to serving others.
Once I have a good sense of myself, my
    needs, and how to nurture myself, I give
    my talents and time to making this world
    a better place.
I do not get hooked into giving to every
    person and cause that crosses my path.
I discriminate between those who
    compliment my need to give and those
    who drain my energy.
I have the ability to say "No" to people and
    causes that do not match up with my
    choice of service.

*I choose a life of service and give from
my overflow.*

True Nurturing

I am the catalyst for others to have a
greater sense of themselves.
I know when to ignite the inner fire of
another and when to let go and watch
the kindled fire begin to blaze on its own.
True nurturing comes from helping others to
discover their own ability to maintain the
fire.
I encourage others to do what I have
learned to do for myself.

---

*I nurture others by recognizing those
who need my spark and those who
simply need encouragement to develop
and sustain their own flame.*

My Importance

My life is important and is much more than
my little self can understand.

It is as if my soul were part of a double helix
in a DNA molecule.

Half of the chain is already in existence as
an expression of the creative Source; my
life then mirrors a small piece of the
chain.

It is comforting for me to know that there is
a bigger, well-thought-out plan for my life
to follow and that I am not blindly
stumbling along.

I dedicate my life to discovering and
exploring my purpose.

*I feel the importance of my special,
unique life.*

Being Stuck

I am in the perfect place on my spiritual
  path at all times.
I let go of the moments when I do not feel
  the light of understanding or forget to
  take care of myself or forget what I knew
  yesterday.
Even when I feel stuck, I observe my actions
  and feelings unemotionally.
If what I am doing is not working, I need to
  turn in another direction.
I forgive myself for being stuck; it is part of
  the process.

When stuck, I look in another direction.

The Way

There is only one way out of my problems,
    dilemmas, and pain.
The way is to live Love... give Love, receive
    Love, express Love, and be Love.
As I allow the Higher Power to use me as a
    channel for unconditional Love, then my
    way is illumined.

I live the way of Love.

My Selves

At times, I feel as if I have different people living inside of me.

Some do not cooperate, some are wise, and some are immature.

It is my job to direct these different aspects of myself to work together.

I facilitate the polar opposites within me; for example, I have the destructive part and the helping part talk and listen to each other.

To deny or suppress a part is to create a roadblock on the path.

This roadblock could come in the form of an illness, an accident, or a person mirroring a suppressed aspect of myself.

I listen to all parts of myself in order to heal and grow into a mature adult.

Positive Intentions

Each immature aspect of me has a positive
  intention.
As I discover the positive intention, I can
  thank that part of me for the job it has
  been doing.
Then, I can talk to it expressing that I want
  to go beyond this present attitude or
  behavior to something more mature.
I continue to communicate with this part of
  me until this immature aspect is willing to
  cooperate and grow to maturity.
I have the ability to heal immature aspects
  of my character with this inner dialogue
  process.

I release immature aspects of myself.

Greater Meaning

I have a choice in how I experience the
   things that happen in my day.
I am learning to totally live from my Higher
   Self and let the Will of Heaven express
   through me.
I do not judge experiences as good or bad.
I look for greater meaning in all the difficult
   things I undergo.
This greater meaning improves the quality
   of my journey.

*I choose to look for greater meaning as
I walk through challenging situations.*

Co-creating

I am connected to all other humans in this
experience of life on this planet.
If I do not like or understand situations that
present themselves in my life, I remember
that we are all learning to be what we
already are...One.
Confusion dissipates when I remember to
co-create reality rather than force my will
or allow another to force their will on me.
I am responsible for part of the outcomes
that manifest when other people are
involved.
Creating reality is shared with others.

I view life from the perspective of co-creating. When two or more of us come together, we share responsibility for creating reality.

Quality of the Journey

I am responsible for my interpretation of
    events that occur in my day.
The quality of my journey is up to me.
I can choose to suffer and get distracted by
    pain, or I can stay centered and
    conscious while undergoing challenging
    lessons.
As I see the big picture, I discover that I no
    longer need to suffer.
I improve the quality of my life by my
    interpretation of events that come my
    way.

*I improve the quality of my journey by
staying conscious and seeing the
patterns of the big picture.*

Patterns

I recognize the negative patterns I learned
    from my family of origin that repeat
    themselves in relationships at work and at
    home.
I transform my current relationship problems
    by first seeing the patterns and then
    spending time pondering the choices I
    have to break out of these patterns.
I attract healthy people and patterns of
    relating when I work on myself first.
I am no longer an unconscious victim.

*I am healing the limiting, crystallized
patterns from the past by working on
my awareness and pondering my choices.*

Improving

My life is improving day by day.
I apply my newly awakened consciousness
    to life situations.
 I see things differently and make new
    choices.
I see the progress I have made and am
    joyfully accepting of myself.
The birth of my new self is steadily
    progressing.
I am optimistic about the future.
I work on today and live it to the fullest.
Tomorrow takes care of itself.
I am peaceful and relaxed as my life
    unfolds.

*Day by day, I see my life improving. I
celebrate the changes I am making and
the peace I am experiencing now.*

Mastering

I am the master of my life.
I take responsibility for my life.
It is no longer a crisis if I make a mistake or a
"wrong" choice.
I will pay the consequences of my choices
and release any critical judgments from
my inner self-talk.
As I grow more aware each day, I realize all
that I have mastered in my life so far.
I continue to step into today to master what
presents itself to me.

I am the master of my life.

Double Agent

I am a double agent.
I live my life from the place of expanded
    awareness; I willingly live in the world.
I can see the patterns and reasons behind
    circumstances that affect my life and do
    not get caught in the drama.
Instead, I tune into my spiritual presence
    and know I am achieving wholeness; it is
    only a matter of time before I am totally
    released from the unpleasant patterns.
I participate in life sharing my new
    awareness only when appropriate.
It is okay that I am aware and that many
    others in my life are not.

---

*I am a double agent for the Source. I
live love without expecting others to
acknowledge me or understand me.*

Teachers

I see a lesson in every experience,
especially the ones that are
uncomfortable.
Each person reflects something about me
that helps transform my consciousness.
I am also the teacher for others, whether
they realize it or not.
I watch the dance between myself and
others.

*I am open and observant to catch the
subtle meaning in all my interactions
with all my teachers.*

Creating as a Process

I create my experiences by seeing my life as
a process.
I stay open to all situations and experiences
as I go through my day.
I see detours that take me off my intended
course as challenges to learn and grow.
Sometimes the rerouting gives me
possibilities for greater growth than might
have been otherwise.

*I create my day by seeing the process of
change as welcome and to be expected.*

Nurturing Myself

I go within to observe and assess my needs
in the four areas of myself: physical,
emotional, mental, and spiritual.
I release the blocks preventing me from
determining my needs.
I am an adult now, and it is okay to say
what I need and want.
I am worthy of getting my needs met.
I am no longer dependent upon others to
meet my true needs.
In my journal, I list all the needs I am
conscious of right now in order to begin
the process of meeting these needs.

*I am worthy of getting my real needs
met. I go within to find out how to
nurture myself.*

Wholeness

My wholeness grows day by day.
No one has to know how deeply I am
    transforming.
If a close friend or family member notices
    that is fine; however, I do not expect
    others to follow my growth.
I share my journey only with others who are
    on a similar path.

I live from my place of wholeness.

Wounds

I continue to heal the wounds from times
  when I was less aware.
I no longer blame others who were unable
  to love and nurture me.
At this moment in time, I acknowledge
  myself for all that it took to get me here.
I am here, now, healing and recovering,
  and that is what is important.

I release past times that wounded me.
I live in the present moment.

Recovery

I realize it takes time to recover from the
    wounds of the past.
I accept the process of recovery.
I allow fellow travelers to show me the way
    when I wander or stray off my path to
    recovery.

---

*I take one step at a time on my path
to recovery.*

Anger

I feel my anger and use its energy to make
    changes and not to blame or hurt myself
    or others.
Choices that I made or others' made
    cannot be changed in the past.
I can use this information, however, to
    create different outcomes today.
I allow the anger to come up and wash
    over my body.
I may need to exercise in order to positively
    use energy created by my anger.

*I listen to my anger, and I use its power
to make positive changes.*

Outer Appearances

I go beyond outer appearances.
I may allow others' behavior to affect me
    until I realize that I have a choice.
Instead of judging another's actions, I look
    within and identify the qualities in me
    that are being reflected.
I cannot attract anything that is not inside
    of me.
The outer reflection allows me to see what is
    disowned within myself.
I use the outer appearances or unconscious
    parts of myself to tell me what I need to
    work on.

*I no longer am deceived by outer
appearances; I recognize them as parts
of myself.*

Polarities Within

I notice polarities within myself.
These opposites give me the challenge to
    learn moderation and blending.
I am a soul experiencing life for growth and
    self-awareness in a system of opposites
    and dualities.
Wholeness is a paradox of being both parts
    of a polarity at the expense of neither.
I accept the opposite parts of myself.
I use the different aspects of myself wisely.

I balance polarities within myself.

Releasing Tension

If I have a clash of wills with other people or a clash with my own inner polarities, I release tension by crying, making loud sounds, exercising, clarifying my thoughts, journal writing, or talking.

It is similar to the calm after a thunderstorm when a new beginning presents itself.

I clear emotional tension when it arises so I can clear away the old and begin anew.

Balance

When I do not feel a sense of balance
within myself, I calmly center myself and
allow the parts of me that need
balancing to blend.
I experience the ups and downs of life and
at the same time maintain my balance.
Like a scale, I move my outer self to
balance the Inner Self.
I am both the Inner Self and the outer self.

*I am balanced and centered as
I experience life.*

Daily Purpose

Today, I live my purpose.
Whatever presents itself to me is what I
    choose to work on.
Rather than wonder what the future
    purpose is, I focus on today.
My purpose may or may not look divine and
    holy; it may look mundane at times.
Going to work or raising a child may be part
    of the plan.
I continue to make myself a better person.
Step by step, I walk the path that is my life.
I am my purpose.

***I feel the purpose of each experience in
my day.***

Choices

I honor the choices my soul made for me to physically experience in my life.

The things that I do not like, I realize, are part of the plan for my life.

I consciously work with all aspects of my life even those that I cannot change and must accept.

I no longer fight the purpose of this life I am living.

I see the Light of Spirit behind the experiences.

Joy spreads over me every time I remember who I really am: a part of the Source growing and transforming.

I honor the choices my soul set in motion for my unfolding of consciousness.

Equilibrium

I move forward with the equilibrium of
balanced motion just as a bird does
when it moves its wings in flight.
This motion of balancing action with
nurturing myself gives me the momentum
to continue my spiritual journey.
Less effort is needed to move when I
maintain my equilibrium.
I do all the things that nurture me so that I
maintain this perpetual motion.

*I easily move forward on the spiritual
path by balancing my actions with
things that nurture me.*

Change

I accept that I am in an ever-changing world.

I connect to Spirit and earth at the same time by visualizing a shaft of light coming from Spirit down through the top of my head, down my spine, and into the center of the earth.

As new experiences continually move into my frame of reference,

I maintain this connection moving forward into a more wondrous experience of my Self.

Change is my friend when I connect to Spirit and matter simultaneously.

Spirit and Matter

I am a unique and incredible being; I am a
combination of spirit and matter.

I am a beam of light—a particle and a
wave all at the same time.

I am an extension of the Source living in a
physical world.

I am also living in emotional, mental, and
spiritual worlds.

I have vehicles for all the dimensions of
my Self.

I am a unique blend of Spirit and matter.

I listen to my neg...
    them into posit...
    them in my jour...
As a healing treatm...
    consciousness, I...
    myself.
I will continue to read...
    the real truth of my be...
My new thoughts guide me...
If I begin the negative self-talk...
    thoughts override.
This is reprogramming my subconsc...
    mind.
This is like putting a new data base into ...
    computer.

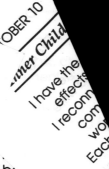

*I put new healthy thoughts into my
mind overriding the old programming.*

power to change the negative
from my past.
ect with my inner child
municating with loving and kind
ds.
day, I ask my child what he/she needs
nd wants.
or example, my inner child is feeling
lonely and withdrawn, I may rock him/her
and listen to inspiring music.
I am always ready to listen to the needs of
my inner child.
I no longer ignore those needs or expect
anyone else to meet them.

*I am responsible for meeting the needs
of my inner child.*

Tolerance

I am tolerant of people who are less aware
than I am.

I practice forgiving them for offensive
behavior and continue to love them at
the impersonal level of mind (this is
unconditional love that the Greeks call
Agape love.)

I, however, make sure I do not set myself up
to be a scapegoat or target.

I consciously decide what I can handle and
what I cannot.

I do not have to continue relating in the
same way if I am not taking care of
myself.

---

*I tolerate people with offensive
behavior. I figure out the best plan for
me to take care of myself.*

Strength

I am strong.
My inner strength allows me to learn from
    whatever happens to me.
It protects me in situations where my
    awareness is limited.
I have the power to take care of myself and
    transform any dark corners that surprise
    me.
I continue my growth and unfoldment
    knowing my strength of character will
    take care of me.

*I have inner strength to meet the
challenges in my life.*

Beauty

I have an inner beauty that radiates and
   shines on all who come onto my path.
I allow this inner beauty to penetrate my
   emotional body.
It feels good to have this strength of inner
   character.
I claim my power to radiate this inner light
   of beauty.

*I am a beautiful expression of the
Godforce. I radiate love and beauty on
all who come into my life.*

Courage

I have the courage to move forward on the
　　path of life.
I am powerful because I know and feel my
　　inner beauty and light.
I meet life with the assurance that all is well
　　and is unfolding for a greater reason and
　　purpose.
I trust the process and have the courage to
　　go into my life fully experiencing all that
　　life has to offer.

*I have the courage to be who I am and
to experience all that my soul has in
mind for me.*

Abundance

The Universe is unlimited; thus I am able to get my needs met.

Conflicting guiding beliefs and needs within me, however, might make it appear that I am not getting what I ask for.

The most dominate need or belief wins when two are in conflict.

It is never Source that deprives me; I do it to myself by having faulty beliefs and false information on how things work.

I can only attract things in the outer world based on my level of awareness.

The creative Source is within me and wants to move me into greater experiences of abundance.

Today, I change at least one unhealthy thought pattern to allow me to receive abundance on the mental plane so that I can manifest it on the physical plane.

I correct false beliefs so that I can have the abundance I deserve.

Materializing

I have the power to materialize what I want.
I am specific about what I want and focus
my mind on it.
As I focus, I begin drawing what I want
towards me.
I pay attention to all negative thoughts that
tell me I do not deserve or cannot have
what I want.
I talk back to this voice with words such as,
"I deserve to have a loving relationship,"
or "I do not have to be perfect to be
worthy of love."
Once I get clear on what it is I want and
change my negative self-talk, I let go,
and the universe brings it to me in correct
timing.

**I am powerful and materialize what I
want and deserve.**

Divine Success

I listen to Spirit when I am creating.
I choose to manifest only what is loving and
    of service to myself or others.
I am successful when I create in
    accordance with my spiritual nature.
Will guided by Spirit brings the ideas of Spirit
    into physical reality.
I spend time meditating and concentrating
    on the true meaning of success, and I
    manifest what my Higher Self has in mind
    for me.

I create divine success in my life.

Heart

My heart opens to the love of Spirit.
It gives me the support I need to heal the
   ruptures in my close relationships.
As I fill myself with the love of Spirit, I am
   renewed and face the difficulties that
   need to be resolved and dissolved.
New patterns of wholeness emerge with the
   opening of my heart center.

***I open my heart to the love and support
of Spirit.***

Letting Go

I leap into the unknown assured of my
success because of the Light I possess.
I trust by letting go of the unreal in my life;
reality will support me.
If others see me as a fool, I remember how I
judged others when I was not mature
enough in consciousness to understand.
Rather than convince or prove my choices,
I quietly progress on the path of
enlightenment.
I no longer need loved ones to understand
my process or come along with me.
I let go of everything that is not in rhythm
with my true destiny.

---

*I let go of everything that holds me in
bondage to what I am not.*

Magic of Spirit

I live with the magic of Spirit.
My life is a channel for this energy.
I simply allow it to flow through me.
I live by letting go moment by moment.
I experience the guidance of the Higher
  Power.
Sometimes this magic is a feeling; at other
  times, it is a vision or a silent voice within.

***I dance with the guidance of the
magical energy of Spirit.***

Secrets

I joyfully hold the secrets of wisdom within
    me.

As I progress on the path of wholeness, I
    experience more and more of what is
    already inside me.

My intellect works with my intuition. I need
    both parts of my mind.

My inner wisdom is understood and put into
    words with the help of my analytical
    mind.

*My Inner Self has all the wisdom to
guide my life. I tune into the secrets of
this inner wisdom.*

Body

My body is healthy and whole.
Each organ and cell works harmoniously as
    a team player with all other parts of my
    body.
I appreciate all the physical parts of me
    and the good job that each part does to
    sustain me.
I tune into my body to find places in need.
I send love and light to any part of my
    system that is hurting.

My body is healthy and whole.

Creativity

I allow my natural creativity to flow through
  me.
I connect with my Higher Self through
  meditation.
Then I use my power of affirmation and
  visualization to manifest in the physical as
  Spirit has guided me.
I express the Love of God when I allow the
  creative Spirit to flow through me.

*I allow the Spirit of creativity to flow
through me.*

Tradition

I honor the traditions of my family and
culture.
I participate to the degree that it feels right
to me.
I use the routine of traditions to order my life.
Traditions anchor me to my past and
provide secure roots.
I evaluate what I want to carry forward in
my life from all the traditions presented to
me.

*I feel safe by honoring and practicing
the traditions that support me in my life.*

Authority

I respect the authority of people in power
who use their power for the greater good
of others.

I notice those who do not have the ability
to lead others and who misuse their
power and authority.

I am conscious of my own authority and
how I affect others.

I am aware of the higher authority I receive
from the Higher Power.

*I listen to the authority of my Higher
Self when I am in positions
of power and authority.*

Union

I accept the union of Spirit and matter into my body awareness.

When I am in this place of grace, I love each person unconditionally.

My special love relationships work easily when I remember all that I am.

As the superconscious mind of the Source enfolds me, the conscious and subconscious parts of my mind are free of separation.

I join all parts of me in oneness.

I am at one with all that I am, and I experience union within myself.

Higher Self

I live my day feeling safe, secure, and
   connected with my Higher Self.
I allow my Greater Self to be in charge of
   my life.
Inner and outer conflicts, as well as physical
   and emotional addictions, no longer rule
   my life.
My Spiritual Self takes charge of my
   personality problems, and I easily live
   with peace and harmony.

I turn my life over to my Higher Self.

Friendship

I care about my friends.
I appreciate the unconditional love and
    emotional support of my close friends.
I express gratitude to those who have
    shared my pain, sadness, joy, and
    excitement.
I send love to people who have shared my
    life with me.

*I appreciate my friends. I lift them into
the Light.*

Purpose

I know I have a purpose.
I am ready to remove the fear of having this
purpose revealed to me.
I have worked diligently on healing my
consciousness and am now ready to
move forward to serve others.
I bring my gift of wholeness into my day and
into my interactions with others.
I am ready to receive the next part of my
spiritual purpose.

*I am open to receiving my next
assignment from Spirit.*

Goodness

Good things are happening in my life.
I watch as my life unfolds with more and
more goodness each day.
I release old hurts and pains, and goodness
finds its way onto my path.
I focus my mind on what is happening in my
day that is good.

*I receive the goodness that I deserve in
my life.*

Death

I honor the time I have on earth today.
I see that the fear of death stops me from a
    true experience of the present.
I allow my fears of death to melt into the
    experiences ahead of me today.
I am alive right now and cherish my life.
I accept that death affects only the
    physical aspects of me.
In Spirit there is no death.

*I embrace the time that I have right
now for loving and learning.*

Transformation

I accept change in my life.
I let go when I reach the place of not
knowing.
I let go of old patterns and behaviors in
order to transform aspects of myself into
greater and greater wholeness.
I am like the caterpillar who is changing into
a butterfly.

**The power of transformation is active
in my life.**

The Golden Mean

I live my life with the intention to experience
   whatever comes my way.
I no longer avoid the positive or negative
   experiences that are presented to me.
I am healing all the misperceptions,
   judgments, and beliefs that took me
   away from the middle path of quiet,
   calm, and peace.
As I trust my process, I choose to experience
   the place of balance that the ancient
   Greeks called The Golden Mean.
I am no longer seduced into the highs or
   lows.
I live joyfully from my heart.
I trust the process.

*By living with inner balance and calm,
I experience the Golden Mean.*

Intuition

I act on my intuition, and divine order
appears in my life.

When I center myself and listen to the quiet,
still voice from within, I have all of the
protection and guidance necessary.

I hear this silent voice whenever I ask for
help.

**I am protected and guided by the power
of intuition.**

Timing

With my inner growth and expansion, I am
aware of the proper timing for me.
I continue to release expectations that are
no longer realistic for me.
I can only respond from my present level of
awareness.
I honor my emotional needs, and I travel at
a comfortable rate along my path.
My goals unfold at the perfect rate for me.
I manage my time and allow my Self to
open like a flower blooming at its perfect
time.

---

*I respond to the proper timing for me to
open and grow.*

Goals

I know the difference between my goals
  and the journey of meeting these goals.
I enjoy the process of life as I meet my
  goals.
I evaluate my goals to see if I have
  outgrown any that were sent forth in less
  aware days.
I take the risks appropriate for today.
I move forward with awareness and self-
  assurance to meet my goals.

*I clearly see and enjoy the journey of
meeting my goals.*

Gardener

I plant new seed thoughts in the garden of
    my mind.
I pull the weed thoughts that interfere with
    my growth.
With loving care, I nurture the new seeds as
    they grow into full stature and beauty
    which reflects the blossoming of Spirit
    within me.

I am the gardener of my consciousness.

Victory

I celebrate the achievements that I
  accomplish.
I rest for a time after reaching a goal in
  order to assimilate the total experience.
I enjoy my process of achieving.
I know when to do and when to be.

*I find joy in the creative process; I
enjoy both the doing and the being.*

Regeneration

I am regenerating my whole being.
As my consciousness changes, all the cells
   in my body get a boost.
Emotionally, I process all of the old stored
   energy of pain and fear in order to
   release me from the bondage of
   physical hurting.
I choose to look straight into old patterns of
   pain and fear, to release them, and to
   regenerate my total self.

I am regenerating my total being.

Others' Choices

I stop controlling other people's choices.
I allow them their learning experiences
    through their achievements, mistakes,
    and experimentations.
I maintain my inner peace when a loved
    one chooses options I deem negative.
I return my focus to myself each time I get
    too involved with another person's
    choices.

*I focus on my life and allow others to
make their own choices.*

Emotional Pain

I no longer criticize myself when I repeat a
negative-feeling emotional pattern.
I realize the repetition allows the intensity to
register an unconscious pattern in my
conscious awareness.
Once emotional pain registers, my mental
self can gather information and try new
things to eliminate the old pattern.
My mental self breaks the emotional prisons
I have created.

---

*I choose new ideas and thoughts to
break my patterns of emotional pain.*

Harmlessness

I practice harmlessness by living my life
without being hurtful to myself or others in
all that I think, say, and do.
I choose to live from the place of right
thinking and right action by listening to
my heart at all times.

I live my life with harmlessness.

Contentment

I am content to be who I am and where I
   am at this moment.
This does not stop my growth; the process of
   living with goals and achievements
   continues.
I take the time, however, to experience the
   joy of all that I have accomplished up to
   this moment.
I am content.

I am content in this moment.

Innate Abilities

I acknowledge my innate abilities and talents that are to be developed and eventually shared.

My special abilities no longer have to stay hidden.

It is never too late to begin appreciating my gifts.

I look at what I have that is unique.

It does not have to be what traditionally is appreciated by society, and it does not have to bring in income.

Developing my special abilities fills me with joy and rounds out my total being.

I develop my special abilities and talents with the sole purpose of rounding out my consciousness.

Family

I appreciate my family.

I look realistically at this group and accept what cannot be changed.

I relate to each member individually and remove myself from conflicts between other members.

I am only responsible for myself in relation to each member individually.

I am brave about bringing up issues that need clarification and healing.

I move in the direction of healthy, loving relationships with all my family members.

I am part of a family. I appreciate this group and my relationship to each person in the group.

Roles

I look at the roles I play in my family, at
   work, and in my close relationships.
I reassess these roles.
Do I want to continue them?
Are any unhealthy for me?
Do I want to create new ones or
   renegotiate old ones?
I evaluate my roles to reflect my inner
   growth at this time.

I am conscious of the roles I play; I take
time to evaluate any changes
I need to make.

Rules

I make a list of the rules by which I live my
    life.
I think about these rules and clarify the ones
    that need to be changed.
I eliminate the ones that are outdated and
    no longer serve me or the greater good.
In their place, I create new rules that
    support my new growth.

*I evaluate and update the rules by
which I live my life.*

Code of Conduct

I write down the code of conduct that
   guides my life.
I become clear what my values are.
I choose to live by the standards that are
   good for me.
Any part of the code that I am unable to
   adhere to is an area for further growth; it
   is the next agenda on my path.

*I live my life with a code of conduct for
my true values.*

Time

Time is my friend.
I work well with time.
I expand time by organizing what I need to
    do and visualizing the most efficient way
    to work.
I compress time by speeding up what I am
    doing.
I use my time wisely.
I balance what I have to do with what I
    want to do.
"Down" time is as important as productive
    time; I live the balance of the two.

Time is my friend.

Friendship

I value my circle of friends.
I connect emotionally with my close friends.
I am there for them, and they are there for
    me.
I share my journey with them and listen as
    they share their journey with me.
Close friends provide an extra measure of
    support and love.
I exchange love and support with my
    friends.

***I value my close friends and share
myself with them.***

Wholeness

I enjoy all of me.
I shine the light of awareness into all my
    spaces to bring any fear, shame, and
    darkness into the open light.
In the light, I heal and feel all of me.
I recognize the parts of me that still need
    attention.
I am willing to go further in my process of
    loving and accepting all that I am.
I experience wholeness when I allow myself
    to be what I am.

*I accept my whole self and know
I am good.*

Higher Will

I have the desire to be all that I truly am.
I trust turning my little will over to the Higher
  Will and Power.
I am a fragment of the Greater Will and
  Power.
I feel light and free when I relieve myself of
  the burden of controlling all that I
  experience.
I am free living from the Higher Will.

The Higher Will guides my living.

Meditation

I live in a continuous meditation.
I talk directly to my Spiritual Self which is
    connected to the Source of all.
I receive direct guidance as I allow this
    power to flow through me.
I take the time to quiet my mind and
    become open to receiving my
    guidance.

I live my day in a continuous
meditation connected to the Source.

Thankfulness

I allow myself to experience the good
 feelings that come from being thankful.
Today, I list all the good things that have
 happened to me, all the people I am
 grateful to have in my life, and all the
 awareness I have had this year.
I focus on what is working and what I do
 have in my life today.
I feel the collective celebration of giving
 thanks from the people in my nation.
I am a part of this group experience.

NOTE: Read this passage on
Thanksgiving Day as the date changes
each year.

I am thankful for my life and all the
opportunities I have to explore and
experience.

Stillness

I experience stillness today to know the
    beauty of my soul.
I listen to the silent voice of inner spiritual
    authority which guides me and shows me
    the way.
Even when my outer world is hurried and
    demands are placed on me, I go in
    peace because I go into the quiet
    stillness that is within.

In stillness, I listen to my soul.

Cooperation

I cooperate with members of my family and
co-workers.

I pay attention to the larger picture; we are
all souls growing in consciousness.

I do not dwell on the difficulty of others'
personalities.

I see that I can make a difference.

I center myself and respond from the place
of maturity.

I limit my reactions and communicate with
skill and deep thought.

I cooperate with others around me.

Silence

Today, I observe my world.
I listen to others and silence my reactive
  mind.
I live with the intention of quieting my mind
  chatter and receiving the guidance my
  Higher Self has for me.
I take the time to slow myself down, to
  practice living with silence, to listen to my
  intuition, and then to act wisely.

I observe my world in silence.

Playfulness

I stop taking myself so seriously today.
I notice when I can lighten up.
I let my inner child play in situations that
    normally stress me.
I cease overworking problems that seem to
    drain me.
I open the door of creativity that was shut
    to my consciousness; I remember to play.

**I unlock the door to my creativity by
being playful.**

Partner

I appreciate my partner (this can be a love
   partner, business partner, roommate,
   etc.) today.
I focus on his or her good qualities.
I mirror love and kindness to my partner and
   help them see their inner beauty and
   light.
I verbalize my appreciation.

***I express gratitude for my
partner today.***

Codependence

I pay attention to my need to be needed.

I give because that is part of my nature and
choose to continue giving.

I am clear, however, about my boundaries
so that I respect my own needs and
have the energy I need to live my life.

I clean up any relationships which have not
supported me or in which I have placed
other's needs before mine.

I get support from others who are also doing
this work.

With honest communication, I confront the
people with whom I am in a
codependent relationship.

*I transform my codependent
relationships to healthy
interdependent relationships.*

Remembering Who I Am

I hold firmly in my mind that I am a part of
   the Universe.
There is no way to stop being part of the
   Grand Plan.
To experience pain at the personality level is
   to grow in consciousness.
I never forget, through all my experiences,
   that I am part of the Source.
Some call me a child of God, others a son
   of God, and others call me a Christed
   being.

---

*I remember who I am at all times so
that I do not buy into the illusion of
separation and confusion.*

Detachment

I watch with detachment as others express
    strong emotions.
When another loses his/her temper, I watch
    with curiosity trying to figure out what is
    happening within that person.
I do not take it personally when another
    looses his/her temper with me.
I am not the cause of such outburst; I am
    only the trigger of something much
    deeper going on with him/her.
I remove myself from people who
    experience rage.
Communication is not possible at that time.
I visualize the other person surrounded by
    light each time they come into my mind.

*I detach from being another
person's target.*

My Body

I love and accept my body.
I release the media's and other people's
images of how my body should look.
I like myself even if my body does not fit
these images set by others.
I talk to my body and tell it, "I love you and
thank you for doing what you do."
My self-esteem is not based on what
appears to be assets or flaws in my body.
I do not compare or make judgments
about other peoples' bodies.

*I see beauty in every body, including
my own.*

Problems

I see my problems as my teachers.
When I need healing and am unaware,
   these teachers present situations that
   look like problems.
A problem simply means I have the
   opportunity to heal the past and
   become more aware.
I gently confront, ponder, and work with
   what I see as problems.
I connect with my Higher Self when I need
   help.
My Higher Self is bigger than any problem I
   can create.

I allow my problems to be my teachers.

Understanding

I like to be understood.
I begin by clarifying my thoughts and
  feelings before I communicate with
  another.
I do this by journal writing, talking into a
  tape recorder, or talking out loud
  imagining that another person is there.
When I understand myself, I communicate
  easily with others.
I also practice understanding others.

*I understand myself, and I
communicate easily with others.*

Addictions

My addictions, whether to a person,
   substance, security, etc., allow me to
   become conscious of my blocks to
   wholeness.

I choose to stop judging myself for past
   behaviors that have allowed the blocks
   to continue.

I transform my addictive behavior, not
   through suppression, but through
   understanding myself and getting my
   needs met.

I honor feelings that were suppressed and
   creative energy that did not know how
   to express itself.

*I allow my addictive behaviors to
show me where I am stuck in the past.
I allow suppressed parts of myself to
express creatively.*

Ego

- I love and appreciate all that the ego (little self) has done to survive.
- I am now ready to submit the ego to the direction of my Higher Self.
- I choose to listen to the quiet voice of the Higher Power.
- My Higher Self steps down the frequency of power so that I can sense, hear, or see this higher truth on a personal level.

I allow my Higher Self to rule my ego.

Senses

I honor my five senses; they help me
     interact with my physical world.
I also honor my sense of intuition that goes
     beyond the physical to connect me with
     the world of Spirit.
I need all my senses, and they are good.

*I appreciate all my senses; they help me
interact with the physical and
spiritual worlds.*

Manifestation

I am capable of manifesting what I need
   and want.
The better I know myself, the wiser I create.
I go within to determine what the true
   desire is, and then I visualize and affirm
   myself manifesting on the physical level.
I feel very deeply the nature of what I want
   to create in order to add power to the
   creating.
Then, I am able to let go and allow the
   Universe to determine the proper timing
   and way of manifesting what I want.

I manifest what is wise and good for me.

Taming My Mind

I master the thoughts and images in my
   mind.
I pay attention to what I am thinking and
   picturing so that I can choose to create
   my highest good.
I focus on the thoughts and pictures that
   support my healing and release those
   that keep me stuck in the past.
I continue to train my mind to be here now,
   without judgment, but with love and
   support.

*I tame my mind in order to create my
highest good and demonstrate
my wholeness.*

Patience

I cooperate with the pace of my healing.
I am patient during confusing times,
    knowing all is in divine order.
I turn inward and remember to focus on the
    task of the moment and not on the goal.
I take deep breaths whenever I lose
    patience because this slows me down
    and balances me in the moment.

---

*I receive patience from my Higher Self
to go through the healing process.*

Resistance

I honor the resistances I sometimes feel to going forward and to making changes.

By giving my time and attention to my resistances, they will show me where I need to place my attention in order to grow.

I do not judge or push myself before I am ready to make changes.

When my discomfort is greater than my resistance, I know I will take the needed steps towards healing.

I honor my resistances. They show me where I need to place my attention in order to grow.

Loving Myself

I practice loving myself.
I do not expect other people to
    unconditionally love me...they may not
    know how. (Remember, a person can
    only love you if they love themselves).
I say kind, supportive things to myself in my
    self-talk.
I choose to love myself when I make a
    mistake or someone else is displeased
    with me.

I feel kind and loving toward myself.

Free to Be

I am free to be my True Self.
I express this Self, and it feels good.
I continue to spend time with myself to
    calmly look inward in order to redefine
    my needs, wants, wishes, hopes, dreams,
    goals, values, and beliefs.
I am not my behavior, thoughts, and
    emotions.
I am the one who behaves, thinks, and
    feels.

I am free to be who I am.

Think

I think about why I do the things that do not
    support my growth.
Today, I study one aspect about myself that
    needs to be changed.
As I discover what the motivation is, I can
    decide rationally how I can do things
    differently.
Since I want different results, I am willing to
    think deeply about aspects of my
    character that interfere with my growth.

*I think about why I do things so I can
solve my problems.*

Boundaries

I choose to have clear boundaries.
I check in with my Inner Self when people
    want me to do something.
The better I listen to my Self, the better I can
    say "yes" or "no" to support myself.
I practice loving myself so that I will have
    the courage to risk rejection by saying
    "no" to things that are not good for me.

*I have the right to say, "no,"
as well as, "yes."*

Good

I know that I am good.
I know that I am at my best when my self-esteem is high.
My intentions are to do, think, and be my best at each moment.
This inner awareness is not dependent on any other person's opinion.
My spiritual essence is the real me.

I know I am good.

Smiling

I smile to express my good feelings and to
  relate with others.
I no longer hide my joy.
I am growing in my ability to love myself.
As my feelings of worthiness grow, it
  automatically shows on my face.
I have a willingness to express on the
  outside the good feelings I am feeling on
  the inside.
Genuine smiles open doors when I relate to
  others.

***I smile to express joy and to open doors
of relating to others.***

Laughter

I laugh at myself often.
I no longer take myself too seriously.
Laughter heals me.
When I lighten up, I make wiser choices and
    handle my mistakes easily.
Laughter helps me express feelings of
    tension and discomfort, as well as joy
    and fun.

I like to laugh at myself.

Deserving

I deserve to feel good, happy, and
confident.
My new level of self-esteem allows me to
have these good feelings.
I remember constantly that I am like the
acorn growing in its perfection to the
mighty oak.
It is never too late to grow strong branches
that were missed earlier.

***I deserve to feel good, happy,
and confident.***

God Within

In the holiday season, I focus on my spiritual
  essence, or God within me.
I go within to listen to my wise Inner Self to
  move in, around, and through all the
  glamour and distractions of the
  commercial outer world.
God speaks to me when I am quiet and
  focused inward.
I take time in my busy day to center myself
  and focus within.

*I listen to God within me to help me
move in the material world.*

Winter Solstice

I go within today to experience the ending
of one cycle and the beginning of a new
one.
The quiet stillness of winter slows me down
and allows my roots of consciousness to
grow to greater depth.
I have spent almost a year focusing on
loving myself.
It is now time to rest and quietly assimilate
what has been gained.

*I go within to feel the ending of a cycle
and prepare for a new birth.*

Teacher Within

I go within to feel the quiet voice of my
   teacher within.
I ask for guidance and insight in order to live
   a fuller life.
My life purpose unfolds as I listen.
I feel a desire to take on greater
   responsibility than I had a year ago.
This past year spent learning to love myself
   from the perspective of my Higher Self
   has given me a fullness that I now want
   to share with others.
I ask my inner teacher to guide me.
I experience the Will of the Source in my life.

I will to will Thy will.

Joy

I feel the joy of the holiday season.
I feel united with the God within.
I feel centered and full.
I no longer feel the separateness from my
    spiritual nature.
I am one with all that is.
I am a channel for love to express through
    me on this earth plane.
I feel the light of day as I continue to
    awaken.
The darkness of being unconscious is behind
    me.

**I am full of joy and spread my light
to others.**

DECEMBER 24

Preparation

I prepare my consciousness for the rebirth.
I spend the day in an active mediation.
Wherever I go, I am tuned into the spiritual
    essence of life.
I release negative programming from past
    experiences and interpretations of the
    holidays.
I attune myself, and I consciously connect
    with each person I meet.
I remember my wholeness and live from my
    fullness.

---

*I prepare my consciousness for
the new birth.*

Christ Consciousness

Today, I am a realized being having
   accepted the rebirth of the higher
   consciousness within my life.
The Christ within me is reborn.
I use the Christmas story to remind me of all
   the parts of myself.
I am my own mother, father, and child.
I am one with the angels and wise men; all
   are part of my consciousness.

*I accept the rebirth of the Christ
Consciousness within me.*

Retreat

I rest and nurture myself today.
I treat myself kindly.
I retreat to build my inner strength; I go
within and review my year.
I notice where I have improved my self-
esteem and where I still need to grow in
awareness.
I make an honest assessment of all my
behavior, thoughts, and feelings.
I write my insights in my journal.

I retreat in strength to review my year.

Future

I write a letter to myself today that I will read
   in one year.
I list everything I want to experience, learn,
   and accomplish in the next year.
I clarify what is practical to achieve in one
   year, taking note of what may be
   unrealistic desires.
This letter of intent will guide me during the
   year.
If I know what the plan is, I can begin
   moving forward on this path.

I make a realistic plan for my next year.

Now

I accept where I am right now on the path
  of life.
By reviewing my year and planning ahead
  for the next, I gently allow myself to feel
  centered right now.
I release judgments of past behaviors which
  I felt were not as positive as they might
  have been.
I steady myself to live from this point in time
  and to be realistic about the pace of my
  growth.
I let go of all unrealistic expectations and
  acknowledge myself for all the growth
  and expansion in awareness I have
  achieved.

I appreciate where I am now.

Awakening

I awaken to the awareness that I am much,
   much more than I thought.
I feel the truth about what my mind has
   been learning this past year.
I feel my spiritual wholeness and my
   connection to the greater plan and
   purpose for me as an individual as well as
   for me as a part of the greater whole.
I am a spiritual being who is waking up to
   my magnificence.

*I awaken to the splendor of my part in
the great plan of the Universe.*

DECEMBER 30

Purification

I prepare myself to join others of like mind in
  World Healing Day which is tomorrow.
I purify myself with proper diet, exercise,
  rest, thought, and meditation.
I prepare myself to be a clear channel for
  Love from the Higher Power.

At noon, Greenwich time,(7:00 a.m.
Eastern Standard Time) on
December 31, I align myself with
people all over the world by reading
the World Healing Meditation on the
next page.

*I purify myself to be a clear channel
of Love.*

World Healing Meditation

In the beginning.
In the beginning *God.*
In the beginning God created the heaven
    and the earth.
And God said Let there be light; and there
    was light.

Now is the time of the *new* beginning.
I am a co-creator with God, and it is a new
    Heaven that comes, as the Good Will of
    God is expressed on Earth through me.
It is the Kingdom of Light, Love, Peace and
    Understanding.
And I am doing my part to reveal its Reality.

I begin with me.
I am a living Soul and the Spirit of God
    dwells in me, as me.
I and the Father are one, and all that the
    Father has is mine.
In Truth, I am the Christ of God.

What is true of me is true of everyone, for
  God is all and all is God.
I see only the Spirit of God in every Soul,
  And to every man, woman and child on
  Earth I say: I love you, for you are me.
You are my Holy Self.

I now open my heart, and let the pure
  essence of Unconditional Love pour out.
I see it as a Golden Light radiating from the
  center of my being, and I feel its Divine
  Vibration in and through me, above and
  below me.

I am one with the Light.
I am filled with the Light.
I am illumined by the Light.
I am the Light of the world.

With purpose of mind, I send forth the Light.
I let the radiance go before me to join the
  other Lights.
I know this is happening all over the world at
  this moment.
I see the merging Lights.
There is now one Light.
We are the Light of the world.

The one Light of Love, Peace and
    Understanding is moving.
It flows across the face of the Earth,
    touching and illuminating every soul in
    the shadow of the illusion.
And where there was darkness, there is now
    the Light of Reality.

And the Radiance grows, permeating,
    saturating every form of life.
There is only the vibration of one Perfect Life
    now.
All the kingdoms of the Earth respond, and
    the Planet is alive with Light and Love.

There is total Oneness, and in this Oneness
    we speak the Word.
Let the sense of separation be dissolved.
Let mankind be returned to Godkind.

Let peace come forth in every mind.
Let Love flow forth from every heart.
Let forgiveness reign in every soul.
Let understanding be the common bond.

And now from the Light of the world, the
   One Presence and Power of the Universe
   responds.
The Activity of God is healing and
   harmonizing Planet Earth.
Omnipotence is made manifest.

I am seeing the salvation of the planet
   before my very eyes, as all false beliefs
   and error patterns are dissolved.
The sense of separation is no more; the
   healing has taken place, and the world is
   restored to sanity.

This is the beginning of Peace on Earth and
   Good Will toward all, as Love flows forth
   from every heart, forgiveness reigns in
   every soul, and all hearts and minds are
   one in perfect understanding.

It is done. And it is so.

For more information, read John Price's
book, *The Planetary Commission*,
available at a bookstore or from The
Quartus Foundation, P.O. Box 1768,
Boerne, Texas 78006-6768, 512/537-4689.

World Healing

I feel peace and joy for the sharing of my
energy in the global mind link for world
peace.
I am part of the critical mass of
consciousness that moves humanity in a
peaceful direction.

*I am one with all minds that join for
world healing and peace.*

A

B

C

H

I

J